OVERVIEW

Overview

Before you can improve your use of time, you need to know how much time you have – typically eight hours in a workday – and how you currently use this time. Keeping a time log for a week and using it to record how long it takes you to complete each of the activities you perform can help you to do this.

You should categorize activities and assign them priority levels so that you can create a summary of how you allocate your time over a typical week. From this summary, you can determine where you are wasting time and then address those areas.

Energy levels fluctuate throughout the day. Knowing how these "peaks" and "valleys" affect your ability to perform certain tasks can help you schedule your tasks in the most effective way.

Generally, energy levels are highest in the morning, so this is a good time to handle difficult or complex tasks that require good short-term memory and high concentration.

In the early afternoon, your energy levels start to drop, so it's best to focus on only moderately demanding tasks. By late afternoon, you have the least energy and should focus on tasks that are the easiest to complete. Afternoons lend themselves to creative tasks, processing information, or drawing on long-term memory.

Energy levels are moderate in the evening, so this is a suitable time for repetitive tasks that require concentration.

The Myers-Briggs test measures your preferences in terms of information gathering, decision making, energy source, and dealing with the outside world to determine your personality type and how you are likely to behave.

These personality traits affect how you manage your time. Each personality type has certain strengths and weaknesses. So knowing more about yourself can help you to determine how to improve your time management skills.

To manage your time and work effectively, you need to start with goals. You need to set goals that are specific, measurable, attainable, realistic, and time-related. Once goals are set, you break them down into tasks to create a comprehensive to-do list. These tasks should be action-centered, incremental, measurable, and scheduled.

Once you know what tasks you need to perform to achieve your goals, you should prioritize each according to its importance and urgency. To do this, you can use a priority matrix, which categorizes tasks as either urgent and important, urgent but not important, not urgent but important, or not urgent and not important.

To prioritize your workload effectively, you can sequence or queue the tasks you need to perform.

Effective Time Management

Sequencing your tasks involves ordering them according to their start dates and the time you have available to complete them. This is most effective for larger tasks. It involves distinguishing between sequential and parallel tasks, scheduling the tasks, and renegotiating deadlines if necessary.

Queuing tasks involves putting them into a specific order of priority. It is most effective when you have conflicting deadlines. You can queue tasks according to their place in line, processing time, due date, or the status or priority of certain customers.

To manage your time effectively, you have to estimate the time it will take to complete each of your tasks. Doing this ensures you can schedule your work appropriately and meet all your deadlines.

To estimate the time frames for your tasks, you can use a simple time frames equation, which uses estimates for the likely, shortest, and longest times to calculate the realistic, shortest possible time that it will take to complete a task.

Benefits of overcoming a habit of procrastinating are that you'll be more productive and less stressed, and that you'll feel more in control of your work.

Strategies for beating procrastination include considering its negative consequences, and identifying and removing any obstacles keeping you from making a start on a task. They also include setting clear deadlines and simply making a start on the work that must be done.

To help overcome a tendency to take on too much work, you should know your core responsibilities and goals, and weigh the importance of assignments in relation to these before agreeing to take them on. You should also schedule your available time. Once you can see that your schedule is full, you'll know not to accept further work.

However, it's often difficult to say "no." It can help to buy time so that you can prepare an appropriate response. Also, you should ensure you refuse a request to take on more work in a way that won't cause offense and that doesn't invite further discussion.

Strategies for reducing the time you spend handling phone calls include delegating the calls to others, shortening the calls, and, when necessary, rescheduling them for once you're less busy.

To reduce the time you spend with drop-in visitors, you can set time limits on discussions, limit the times for which you're known to be available, immediately ask any visitor how you can help, and encourage visits outside your workplace.

CHAPTER I - ANALYZING YOUR USE OF TIME

CHAPTER I - Analyzing Your Use of Time

At one time or another, you've probably felt that there's just not enough time in the day to get everything done. It can be frustrating and exhausting to feel like this. So how do you find time for all the things you need to do? Before you can really manage the time you have, you need to understand what you're doing with your time now. Begin by asking yourself two basic questions: "How much time do I have?" and "How do I spend my time?"

Creating a time log is a good first step in gaining control over your time. To do this, you should keep a daily log for a week, categorize the activities you perform, prioritize these activities, and then summarize the data you obtain.

Once you have a summary of your logged time for a week, you can begin to assess how effectively you're using the time you have. You can identify your main time wasters and, from there, decide what actions to take. It may be that you should be delegating some of your tasks or giving more time to others.

Are you better able to deal with complex problems in the morning? Do you prefer to work at reflective or creative tasks in the afternoon? It's common to feel ebbs and flows of energy throughout the day. They're a result of changes in your body clock.

If you can match the activities you need to do to times when you are best able to do them, you will be more effective and productive in carrying out those activities.

Do you know what type of personality you have and how it might influence your use of time? Personality can definitely affect how you use your time, so it may help to do a personality assessment.

The Myers-Briggs psychological personality measure is an established personality assessment tool. It measures psychological preferences in four areas – the source of your energy, how you gather information, how you make decisions, and how you deal with the outer world.

Your personality type can help you determine your strengths and weaknesses in terms of time management. The most important personality dimension in this regard is your preference as an extravert or introvert. However, your preferences as a sensor or intuitive, thinker or feeler, and judger or perceiver also impact how you use your time.

If you have a preference for introversion, you likely work best when not distracted by others. You can stay focused on a single task for lengthy periods.

WHY USE A TIME LOG?

Why use a time log?

At one time or another, you've probably felt that there's just not enough time in the day to get everything done. It can be frustrating and exhausting to feel like this. So how do you find time for all the things you need to do? Before you can really manage the time you have, you need to understand what you're doing with your time now. Begin by asking yourself two basic questions: "How much time do I have?" and "How do I spend my time?"

See each question for more information about how to answer it.

How much time do I have?

Answering how much time you have is easy when it comes to a typical workday. You usually have eight hours in which to get your work done, with a further hour for lunch. However, this may vary depending on your job or the organization where you work.

How do I spend my time?

Finding out how you use your time at work is more complicated than finding out how much time you have.

For example, do you know how much time you spend on the phone? Answering e- mails? Writing reports? Or waiting for your computer to boot up?

To get a clear idea of how you use your time, you may find it useful to create a detailed log of the way you spend the hours in your workday.

You might consider using a time log to track the activities you spend time on during a typical week. You should include how long each activity lasts, as well as its priority in relation to your goals.

Recording and assessing your use of time in a time log will benefit you. Using a time log helps you to clarify how you use your time so you can identify any problem areas. You can then determine how best to change what you do so that you use your time more productively.

A time log shows you how much time you're really spending on activities that don't help you meet your goals. So it identifies problem areas in the way you manage your time and indicates changes you can make to be more productive. The information it provides places you in control, equipping you to manage your time better in the future.

When you feel in control, you experience less stress and are more relaxed. In turn, you feel better about yourself and are more productive and motivated. So, ultimately, the quality of your life can improve as you take control of your time.

HOW TO CREATE A TIME LOG

How to create a time log
Creating a time log is a good first step in gaining control over your time. To do this, you should keep a daily log for a week, categorize the activities you perform, prioritize these activities, and then summarize the data you obtain.

See each step for more information about it.

Keep a daily log
Generally, keeping a daily log for a full working week will provide sufficient data to work with. It's important to record every activity right after you've completed it. If you don't, you may forget what you've done and you'll be guessing at how long it took.

You should include even minor activities, such as tidying your desk and taking coffee breaks. Each of these activities takes up time and would be difficult to remember if you tried to create the log from memory at the end of a day.

Ideally, the log should cover typical days rather than days that include an unusual amount of travel, long meetings, or other atypical events.

Categorize activities

As you enter each activity in the log, try to label it using specific categories such as "e-mail," "paperwork," "break," or "meeting."

By creating these categories, you'll provide a simple framework that makes it easier to analyze your log later.

Prioritize activities

You should prioritize activities based on their urgency and importance in relation to your main responsibilities and goals. For example, you might assign the letter "A" or "H" for high to priorities that involve your critical goals and responsibilities.

The next set of priorities involve enabling goals – activities that indirectly support your critical goals. These activities have a medium value and a high degree of urgency. You could label them "B" or "M" for medium.

The lowest priorities include both urgent and nonurgent tasks that have little value in relation to your goals.

Summarize data

At the end of the week, you should summarize the data you've gathered, adding up the total amount of time you spent on each activity category.

You should include the total number of hours spent on each category, the average time per day, and the priority given to that category.

Sally McMahon is a purchaser for a fashion house. Her key responsibilities are to negotiate with suppliers for stock and to ensure stock matches fashion trends.

Effective Time Management

Sally is battling to keep up with her work, so she decides to create a time log to assess where all her time is going. Follow along as she uses the four steps to create a time log.

As soon as Sally completes each activity, she jots down the time and a brief description of what the activity involved.

Sally's time log consists of a table with five columns and nine rows. The columns are headed time, category, activity, priority, and minutes. In the first row, the time is 8:00, the activity is reading and writing e-mails, work-related, and the minutes are 15. In the second row, the time is 8:15, the activity is planning the day's schedule, and the minutes are 10. In the third row, the time is 8:25, the activity is met with new recruits, and the minutes are 40. In the fourth row, the time is 9:05, the activity is negotiating with suppliers, and the minutes are 30. In the fifth row, the time is 9.35, the activity is team-building exercise and the minutes are 90.

In the sixth row, the time is 11:05, the activity is reading and collating sales analysis documents to see what stock is needed, and the minutes are 68. In the seventh row, the time is 12:13, the activity is researching fashion trends online, and the minutes are 50. In the eighth row, the time is 1:03, the activity is lunch, and the minutes are 57. In the ninth row, the time is 2:00, the activity is traveling to see potential suppliers and their stock, and the minutes are 30.

Next Sally assigns a category to each activity. The main categories she identifies are e-mail, planning, meetings, analysis, research, lunch, and travel.

In the first row, the category is e-mail. In the second row, the category is planning. In the third row, the category meeting. In the fourth row, the category is meeting. In the fifth row, the category is meeting. In the sixth row, the category is analysis. In the seventh row, the category is research. In the eighth row, the category is lunch. In the ninth row, the category is travel.

She also assigns a priority to each activity. She decides to use "H" to identify top priorities, "M" for medium-priority activities, and "L" for low-priority activities. When setting priorities for her activities, Sally considers their value and urgency in relation to her goals. For example, a critical goal for Sally is to negotiate with suppliers for the best deals for her company.

In the first row, the priority is M. In the second row, the priority is H. In the third row, the priority is L. In the fourth row, the priority is H. In the fifth row, the priority is L. In the sixth row, the priority is H. In the seventh row, the priority is H. In the eighth row, the priority is set to L. In the ninth row, the priority is set to L.

At the end of the week, Sally summarizes the data about the time she has spent on each category of activities. She then places each category in order of time spent. The summary shows that she spends most of her time in non-essential meetings.

Sally's summary for the week of 1 June is made up of a table with four columns and nine rows. The colums are headed activity, total hours, average per day, and priority. In the first row the activity is non-essential meetings, the total hours are 12:30, the average per day is 2:30, and the priority is L. In the second row the activity is analysis, the total hours are 07:30, the average per day is 1:30, and the

Effective Time Management

priority is H. In the third row the activity is research, the total hours are 05:30, the average per day is 1:06, and the priority is H. In the fourth row the activity is essential meetings, the total hours are 05:00, the average per day is 1:00, and the priority is H. In the fifth row the activity is telephone, the total hours are 02:30, the average per day is 00:30, and the priority is M. In the sixth row the activity is breaks, the total hours is 02:30, the average per day is 00:30, and the priority is L. In the seventh row the activity is travel, the total hours are 02:00, the average per day is 00:24, and the priority is L.

In the eighth row the activity is e-mail, the total hours are 02:00, the average per day is 00:24, and the priority is M. In the ninth row the activity is planning, the total hours is 00:50, the average per day is 00:10, and the proprity is H.

Sally can use the summary she created to analyze how she spends her time. For example, does she spend too much time on low-priority tasks? And how much time does she spend on tasks directly related to her main goals?

Recording and summarizing how she uses her time will help her answer these questions. She can then determine what her main time wasters are and eliminate them.

Question

Taku is a sales consultant for a medical supply company. His primary goal is to generate sales. His main responsibilities are to establish and maintain customer relationships. He also needs to prepare action plans to identify specific targets and to project the number of contacts to be made.

Which statements apply to his log?

Access the learning aid Taku's Time Log to help you answer the question.

Options:

1. The activities are categorized to make it easier to analyze the log later

2. The priority assigned to checking phone messages is high because it relates to one of Taku's main responsibilities

3. Taku shouldn't include minor activities such as taking breaks in his log

4. Taku can use the information from his daily log to create a summary log

5. Taku should assign priority ratings only to his most important tasks

Answer:

Option 1: This is a correct option. Categorizing activities is an important step towards analyzing the log. It will enable Taku to summarize his findings so he can determine how much time he spent on different types of activities.

Option 2: This option is correct. It's vital that Taku follows up on all his phone messages from customers in order to maintain customer relationships. Because this activity relates to one of his key goals, he assigns it a high priority in the time log.

Option 3: This is an incorrect option. To get a clear idea of how he spends his time, Taku needs to record every activity he performs, including those that seem minor.

Option 4: This option is correct. At the end of the week, Taku should summarize the data he has gathered, adding up the total amount of time he spent on each category of activities. He can then use this summary to determine how he is spending most of his time.

Option 5: This option is incorrect. It's important to prioritize each activity, so that at the end of the week you can more easily see whether you are spending time on the activities that are most important for meeting your goals. These include medium-priority activities as well as those with high priority. If you include low-priority activities as well, you'll be able to determine if you are spending too much time on time.

DETERMINING TIME WASTERS

Determining time wasters

Once you have a summary of your logged time for a week, you can begin to assess how effectively you're using the time you have.

You can identify your main time wasters and, from there, decide what actions to take. It may be that you should be delegating some of your tasks or giving more time to others.

For example, Sally seems to be spending too much time in non-essential meetings.

Examples of common time wasters include focusing on the wrong tasks, failing to delegate, misjudging how much time an activity will take, procrastinating, and socializing too much.

See each common time waster for more information about it.

Focusing on the wrong tasks

You may find some tasks enjoyable or feel pressured to carry out other tasks that don't help you reach your goals. You may also underestimate the time you spend on these tasks. For example, you may think that you spend only a little time surfing the Internet and answering personal e-mails, but in reality this may take up several hours of your time each week.

Alternatively, you may spend a lot of time in unnecessary meetings or with unscheduled visitors to avoid being seen as rude. Then you may end up having to take work home to finish it by a deadline.

Failing to delegate

You may find that you're short on time because you do other people's work instead of managing their efforts, or because you enjoy being someone who others rely on in a crunch. If much of your time is spent helping others or doing work that isn't directly linked to your critical goals, you are probably failing to delegate.

The more you do that which is not leading toward your critical goals, the less time you have to complete work that's really important, and the more stressed you will become.

Misjudging time

If you misjudge how long a task will take, you may find that you spend a lot of time waiting for something to happen before you can continue working. So if your time log has long periods of waiting, or if you note that you are consistently late, you know that you have been misjudging time.

You may also schedule too many tasks in a day and end up having to take work home to meet a deadline. So if your time log includes take home work, misjudging time may be one of your time wasters.

Procrastinating

You may procrastinate, or find yourself putting important things off until later. This can take the form of focusing on business tasks that aren't urgent or of doing things that aren't business- related at all – such as surfing the Web or going through personal e-mail.

If you spend large parts of your day on medium- or low-priority tasks and only a small amount of time on high-priority tasks, it may be because you're procrastinating.

Socializing

Some jobs require you to be sociable. For example, you may need to spend time developing relationships with clients or employees. However, people often misjudge just how much time they spend socializing.

If you are spending large amounts of time socializing, you may battle to complete critical tasks, with the result that you feel overwhelmed and stressed.

Tina's summary time log indicates that she may be losing valuable hours to some common time wasters. Her main responsibilities are to design and create images for web site animations, and to resolve problems when they occur. Her goal is to complete her animation projects within the deadlines.

Tina often spends time waiting for the Marketing Department to decide on the parameters for a design. When this happens, she often socializes with colleagues or – via e-mail or the phone – other friends.

She also spends too much time on research and on casual meetings, which are of low priority.

In fact, an analysis of the log indicates that she spends more than half of her working week on low-priority tasks.

Effective Time Management

Tina is not spending enough time doing the things that relate to her goals and responsibilities – namely, designing and problem solving.

She spends only ten hours a week designing animations, and two-and-a-half hours a week on problem solving.

She should look into ways to use her time more effectively.

Once you have identified your own time wasters by analyzing your summary time log, you can begin to develop strategies for avoiding them so that you use your time more effectively.

Question

Remember Taku, who's a sales representative for a medical supplies company? His primary goal is to generate sales. His main responsibilities are to establish and maintain customer relationships. He also needs to prepare action plans to identify specific targets and to project the number of contacts to be made.

Access the learning aid Taku's Weekly Summary to help you determine which statements about how Taku spends his time are correct.

Options:

1. Taku spends too much time socializing

2. Taku spends a lot of time traveling in order to reach his goal of generating sales

3. Taku could be procrastinating because he spends almost an hour a day socializing

4. Taku should delegate some of his customer relations activities to use his time more effectively on planning

5. Taku should not have set planning as a high-priority task because he doesn't spend much time on it

Answer:

Option 1: This option is correct. Socializing is a low-priority task, but Taku spends more than four and a half hours a week doing this. It could be that he is procrastinating – which is one of the most common time wasters.

Option 2: This option is correct. Taku needs to travel to meet customers and make sales. One of his main responsibilities is maintaining good customer relations.

Option 3: This is a correct option. Socializing could be how Taku puts off uninteresting tasks. He needs to think about why he is socializing so much and consider ways to use his time more effectively.

Option 4: This option is incorrect. Taku does need to spend more time on planning, which is a high-priority task. However, handling customer relations is central to Taku's responsibilities and it wouldn't be

appropriate for him to delegate this high-priority task to others. Coordinating shipping schedules and delivery – a low-priority task – might be something Taku could delegate.

Option 5: This option is incorrect. Taku should assign priorities to activities based on his job responsibilities and goals, and planning is one of his main responsibilities. In fact, he should be spending more time on it rather than changing its priority.

Question

You have learned how to create a time log and to use it in assessing how you spend your time.

Which are benefits of being able to do this?

Options:

1. You'll be able to avoid time-consuming tasks in the future

2. You'll be able to pinpoint the kinds of changes you need to make

3. You'll be able to identify any problem areas

4. You'll have a clearer understanding of what your main responsibilities are

5. You'll have greater control of your time

Answer:

Option 1: This is an incorrect option. Reviewing how you spend your time doesn't mean that you will be able to avoid time-consuming tasks. Some tasks just take a lot of time.

Option 2: This option is correct. Once you've recorded how you're currently spending your time, you can identify your time wasters and determine what changes you need to make to work more productively.

Option 3: This option is correct. Recording how you spend your time will show you if you are spending too much time on low-priority tasks – or not enough on tasks that have high priority.

Option 4: This option is incorrect. You should know your main responsibilities before you assess how you spend your time. Your goals and responsibilities will guide you in setting the priorities of the activities you include in a time log.

Option 5: This option is correct. Understanding how you are currently spending your time and why equips you to manage your time better in future.

YOUR BODY CLOCK AND PERFORMANCE

Your body clock and performance

Are you better able to deal with complex problems in the morning? Do you prefer to work at reflective or creative tasks in the afternoon? It's common to feel ebbs and flows of energy throughout the day. They're a result of changes in your body clock.

Question

Understanding how your body clock affects your performance can help you to manage your time more effectively. Your circadian rhythm, or body clock, influences your ability to perform tasks effectively throughout the day.

When do you think you are most alert?

Options:
1. Morning
2. Early afternoon
3. Late afternoon

Answer:

Effective Time Management

Option 1: Your rhythm matches that of most people. It's pretty common to feel most alert in the morning, after you've shaken off the initial grogginess after waking up.

Option 2: Your rhythm is fairly unusual. Most people feel sharpest in the morning and least alert in the early afternoon.

Option 3: It's common for people to experience a rise in energy during the late afternoon and evening, but most people report feeling at their most alert in the morning.

Typically, an individual's circadian rhythm follows a general pattern. Of course, people are different, and you may describe yourself as a "morning person" or a "night person." But everybody's clock settles into a pattern of alertness, followed by dipping energy, and then energy recovery.

Once you know the typical pattern of energy flow, you may want to schedule your tasks a little differently.

The circadian rhythm chart's x-axis represents the time of day, and the y-axis represents the different energy levels going up to one hundred. In the morning your energy level is at its highest, one hundred. In the afternoon, your energy levels drop to close to zero, and in the evening they rise again to fifty.

Examples of tasks are research the proposal, finish the calculations for the proposal, write the first draft of proposal, meet with accounting regarding proposal, finish updating schedule, go to gym, and data entry.

It's true you may not always be able to control the timing of your tasks.

But for tasks within your control, it can be helpful to consider your natural energy rhythms when scheduling them.

SCHEDULING BASED ON ENERGY CYCLES

Scheduling based on energy cycles
If you can match the activities you need to do to times when you are best able to do them, you will be more effective and productive in carrying out those activities.
Question
Typically, when do you think would be the most effective time to make an important decision?
Options:
1. Morning
2. Early afternoon
3. Late afternoon

Answer:
Morning is usually the best time to make important decisions. This is when you are at your sharpest and can deal most effectively with complex issues. Your energy dips in the afternoon, so you should avoid decision making then. The afternoon is better for tasks that require some reflection. And in the evening, although your energy

levels increase again, you still aren't as alert as in the morning. It's best to take on more routine tasks then.

Option 1: This is the correct option. Most people enjoy their greatest level of alertness during the morning.

Option 2: This option is incorrect. Most people experience an energy slump in the early afternoon, and this affects their ability to process complex information.

Option 3: This option is incorrect. Late afternoon is usually when people are less alert.

It can be useful to break time into several categories when determining when to schedule tasks based on your energy cycle – for instance, morning, early afternoon, late afternoon, and evening.

See each time period to find out which tasks are best suited to different parts of the working day.

Morning

The morning is best used for decision making and intellectually challenging tasks. Your energy levels are at their highest and you're alert, so you're able to "think on your feet" and handle difficult or complex issues.

You should try to schedule meetings or conference calls for this time of the day. You should also focus on reading and analyzing information, problem solving, and getting to grips with difficult issues.

Early afternoon

Most people's energy levels begin to dip in the early afternoon. During this time – say from around 12:30 p.m. to 2:30 p.m. – you should avoid mentally challenging tasks or activities requiring active short-term memory and quick thinking.

At this time of day, you generally have the highest tolerance for pain. So this is an ideal time to visit the dentist or chiropractor, or to schedule other appointments that might involve discomfort.

Late afternoon

Energy levels are generally at their lowest during the late afternoon - from around 3 p.m. up to 4:30 p.m. You should not attempt to do anything mentally taxing, such as problem solving, calculations, or attending meetings, at this time. Instead, concentrate on reflective and creative tasks.

This may include thinking about issues, writing, processing information, preparing for speeches or presentations, or anything that involves using your long-term memory.

Evening

As evening begins, most people find that their energy levels begin to increase. But although your energy levels are recovering, you usually aren't as alert as you were at the beginning of the day.

This is the time to undertake routine or repetitive work that requires concentration but not analytical skills. Focus on tasks such as filing, making follow-up calls, checking documentation, or capturing data. This is also a good time to do physical exercise.

Because designing animations takes a lot of concentration and is her most important responsibility, Tina schedules this task for the morning. This is also the time she uses to brainstorm new design ideas with the team.

In the afternoon, Tina schedules problem-solving tasks and sometimes trains the team in technical processes.

In the late afternoon, she usually goes back to design work to try to catch up. She also organizes files and strategies for the next day.

Do you think Tina is making the best use of her natural energy cycle? Actually, she could make some changes to her schedule to take better advantage of this cycle.

For example, she should solve problems, design difficult animations, and train people in the morning, because all these tasks require high levels of concentration. Brainstorming ideas and filing should be rescheduled for the early afternoon because they require less concentration.

She can leave her late afternoons as they are, doing the simpler animations during this time.

Question

Match each task to the time of day during which it is best completed according to the natural energy cycle.

More than one task can be assigned to a particular time of day.

Options:

A. Analyzing sales figures
B. Dealing with a difficult client
C. Updating weekly project reports
D. Visiting the dentist
E. Writing a speech

Targets:

1. Morning
2. Early afternoon
3. Late afternoon
4. Evening

Answer:

It's best to analyze sales figures and to deal with difficult clients in the morning. Typically, your energy level is at its highest in the morning, making it a good time to deal with difficult and complex tasks.

Energy levels begin to flag in the early afternoon, so this is not a good time to focus on mentally challenging tasks. However, at this time of the day, people have the highest tolerance for pain, so it's a good time to visit the dentist.

Energy levels are lowest during the late afternoon. During this time, it's best to focus on creative tasks, drawing on long-term memory, or processing information, so it's a good time to write a speech.

Updating weekly project reports is a task suitable for the evening. Energy levels are increasing, and it's a good time for routine or repetitive work that requires concentration.

PERSONALITY TYPES

Personality types

Do you know what type of personality you have and how it might influence your use of time? Personality can definitely affect how you use your time, so it may help to do a personality assessment.

The Myers- Briggs psychological personality measure is an established personality assessment tool. It measures psychological preferences in four areas – the source of your energy, how you gather information, how you make decisions, and how you deal with the outer world.

See the areas to find out which preferences apply to them.

Source of your energy

Where people place their attention and what energizes them varies along a scale between extraversion and introversion. These words have a particular sense when used in psychology. And they are sometimes referred to as attitudes.

Those who are extraverted prefer to spend their time focusing on people and things. They draw their energy from action. Introverts, on the other hand, draw energy from the inner world of concepts and ideas. They tend to build energy by reflecting, rather than acting.

You may find that you spend some time being extraverted and some being introverted. This is the norm. And you shouldn't confuse introversion with shyness or reclusiveness because they are not necessarily related.

How you gather information

How people prefer to take in information varies along a scale between sensing and intuition.

If you prefer sensing as a way of understanding and interpreting new information, you are likely to trust information that is in the present, tangible, and concrete – in other words, information that comes from your five senses.

Conversely, intuition refers to gathering information by examining patterns and considering possibilities from the information you receive. It is a more theoretical and abstract process than sensing.

How you make decisions

Thinking and feeling are the two functions you use to make decisions. These terms, as used in psychology, shouldn't be confused with being intelligent or emotional. Both thinking and feeling can be used to make rational decisions, drawing on data received through information gathering.

People who prefer thinking tend to make decisions based on general rules and facts. They take a more detached position, focusing on what appears reasonable, logical, and consistent.

People in the feeling category prefer to make decisions based on personal concerns and the people involved in the context of the decisions.

How you deal with the world

When dealing with the outer world, people have a preference for using either the judging or perceiving function.

Judging means you prefer a more structured way of relating to the world. It doesn't mean you are judgmental. Perceiving means you have a more flexible or adaptable way of relating to the world.

People who have a preference for judging tend to want things settled or decided, and focus on making decisions. Those with a preference for perceiving focus more on taking in information. Here, being perceptive doesn't mean having quick and accurate perceptions about people and events – it means you prefer taking in information or weighing facts over having final decisions.

Review each personality preference for more information about it.

Extraversion

Extraverts find energy by being actively involved in a variety of group activities. They like to make things happen and to energize others.

They generally feel at home in public and often understand problems better when they talk about them and listen to what others have to say.

Introversion

Introverts find energy from working with ideas, images, memories, and internal reactions – they are energized by their internal world.

They prefer working alone or in very small groups, and tend to take time to reflect before taking any action.

Sensing

People whose preference is for sensing pay attention to what they can see, hear, touch, smell, or taste.

Physical data and facts are how they gather information. They wouldn't trust hunches that seem to come out of nowhere, but instead look for facts and details. They tend to remember details that are important to them and focus on what is actual, real, and present. They also focus on the practical use of information.

Intuition

People who gather information by intuition tend to focus on patterns and impressions inferred from their experiences. They prefer to theorize first rather than learning through a hands-on approach. If you are a person that relies on your intuition, you may be more interested in future possibilities than in the present. And you may trust hunches.

Intuitives also tend to remember their experiences more as impressions than as detailed events.

Thinking

When making decisions, people whose preference is for thinking try to base their decisions on principles, facts, and rules rather than on the specific contexts in which they are making the decisions.

Thinkers weigh up pros and cons and then try to be logical and consistent in how they use that information to make decisions. Typically, thinkers focus on being objective rather than taking their own or others' feelings into account.

Feeling

People who prefer to make decisions using feeling as a guide rely on values rather than facts and principles. They weigh the views and needs of the people involved in the specific context of any situation.

Feelers try to establish or maintain harmony and do so by considering the points of view of those involved. They often appear caring and tactful. However, they can also be perceived as too idealistic and as being indirect because of their preference for being tactful over telling the "cold" truth.

Judging

Judgers are people who like to reach clear decisions as quickly as possible. They are task- oriented. And they often feel a need for structure and organization when dealing with the external world. Others may interpret this as being too rigid or controlling.

Judgers prefer to have a plan in place and to keep things in order. They may feel a strong urge to bring life under control.

Perceiving

Perceivers relate to the external world by trying to understand and adapt to it moment by moment. Unlike judgers, they prefer not to reach final decisions, but rather to remain open to new information.

This may result in others seeing them as indecisive or too easy going.

People with this way of relating to the world feel most comfortable when being flexible and spontaneous. Perceivers are more motivated by the desire to understand and respond to the world than by the urge to organize it.

With the Myers-Briggs personality test, you're assigned a particular personality type once your preference in each category has been determined. This personality type is expressed as a code with four letters. In total, there are 16 possible combinations of preferences within the four categories identified by the test.

Suppose Tina takes the Myers-Briggs test and finds that she is an ISTJ personality type. This indicates her preferences are introversion, sensing, thinking, and judging.

Note

For a professional analysis of your personality type, you will need to take the Myers-Briggs test with the help of a professional. An analysis done on your own is unlikely to give you a reliable result.

Tina is likely to be an original thinker who reaches her own conclusions and acts independently. Once committed to a plan, she tends to be highly motivated. She sees things through and strives for concrete results.

Tina is probably a good organizer, with a broad perspective. She can make long-term plans and take many factors into account. In addition, Tina's personality type implies that she sets high standards for others as well as for herself.

Question

Match examples of preferences to the personality traits to which they apply.

Options:

A. Likes to plan ahead and have matters settled

B. Likes flexibility and being open to new information

C. Turns inward for inspiration; reflects before acting

D. Feels it's important to be objective and know the facts before making choices

E. Trusts hunches; is interested in the big picture rather than finer details

F. Starts with facts and forms a big picture; doesn't rely on hunches in decision making

Targets:
1. Judger
2. Perceiver
3. Introvert
4. Thinker
5. Intuitive
6. Sensor

Answer:

Judgers like to have plans and systems in place before proceeding.

Perceivers like to react spontaneously to situations and are open to change and new information.

Introverts are inspired by ideas, images, and theories and typically prefer working on their own or in small groups. They like to have time to think about situations before they take action.

Thinkers like to approach situations logically and value impartiality.

Intuitives tend to focus on patterns rather than on particular details, and often rely on hunches when making decisions.

Sensors are practical in their approach and like to look for facts before forming opinions. They generally do not form opinions based on hunches.

PERSONALITY AND TIME MANAGEMENT

Personality and time management

Your personality type can help you determine your strengths and weaknesses in terms of time management. The most important personality dimension in this regard is your preference as an extravert or introvert. However, your preferences as a sensor or intuitive, thinker or feeler, and judger or perceiver also impact how you use your time.

If you have a preference for introversion, you likely work best when not distracted by others. You can stay focused on a single task for lengthy periods.

However, you might forget to confirm plans with others or fail to find out what's actually happening around you and so overlook new developments.

If you show a preference for extraversion, you probably like to plan and come up with ideas as part of a group. You enjoy keeping busy and working on several projects at once, and you thrive on plenty of stimulation. However, you may have a tendency to jump too quickly into a task, not planning or thinking it over enough. You may also forget to stop and clarify what you want to do and why when you're starting a project or task.

If you prefer sensing to intuition, you like working with schedules and deadlines because you tend to be practical and goal-oriented. However, you may focus too much on present tasks and therefore fail to plan thoroughly. You may also forget to take other people into account when making your plans because you are so focused on the tasks ahead.

If you prefer intuition, you are good at seeing the big picture, so planning may come naturally to you. However, your tendency to remember impressions rather than details means that you may not plan in enough detail.

You trust impressions, symbols, and metaphors more than what you have experienced, so you may miss things when planning. Because you tend to think more about new possibilities and ideas, you may forget to consider how to make them a reality. This may slow you down at work and mean that you struggle with deadlines.

Those with a preference for thinking tend to emphasize being objective and consistent. You may like to break things down into their logical parts, which can help when you're planning.

If you're a thinker, you may be capable of creating very efficient time management systems based on a rational, objective assessment of your goals.

If you have a preference for feeling over thinking, you like to make decisions based on how they affect others and yourself. This may result in your finding protocols stifling or frustrating. And it may cause you to be slow in making decisions, particularly if you want to please all sides.

Because your focus is on other people, you may be easily distracted if you don't have a time management plan.

If your personality includes a preference for judging, you may have a natural flair for time management because planning is important to you. You prefer a more structured way of relating to the world so you do well with schedules and deadlines, and often find planning on paper useful.

A preference for judging can also indicate that you like to complete your work before relaxing and don't like to leave tasks to the last minute. You tend to make lists of things to do and like to plan your work to avoid having to rush just before it's due. However, you may ignore new information because you have not planned for it in advance, or because you are too focused on your goals.

If you have a preference for perceiving, you may find too much planning annoying and restrictive. You like to stay open to respond to whatever happens and keep plans to a minimum. You value flexibility, enjoy mixing work and play, and feel motivated by approaching deadlines. You work in short bursts of energy, rather than at a steady pace. However, you may find that you stay open to new information for too long and therefore don't make decisions when they are needed.

Question

Which statements about how people's preferences affect their approaches to time management are true?

Options:
1. A judger likes to get work done before relaxing
2. An extravert likes comprehensive, predictable plans
3. A perceiver values flexibility when creating plans
4. A thinker likes to plan logically to meet specific goals

5. An introvert needs to multi-task to stay focused

6. A feeler may be reluctant to make quick decisions

Answer:

Option 1: This option is correct. Judgers like to get work done before relaxing because they generally need things to be in order first.

Option 2: This option is incorrect. Extraverts generally like to multi-task and have flexible plans.

Option 3: This option is correct. Perceivers value flexibility in their plans so that they are free to respond to changing situations.

Option 4: This option is correct. Thinkers are usually logical and goal-oriented, and like to plan accordingly.

Option 5: This option is incorrect. Introverts need time alone to process information, and can often work on a single task for long periods.

Option 6: This option is correct. Feelers like to consider how their decisions will affect other people and try to please them, rather than rushing into decisions.

Whatever combination of traits you have, you'll tend either toward over-managing your time or toward simply dealing with matters as they arise. If you like to control your time, you may need to become more flexible. And if you tend to favor spontaneity, you probably need to gain more control over your work schedule.

See each personality trait for more specific advice on how to manage your time.

Extravert

If you're extraverted, you tend to plan while in meetings, so you may find portable planning devices, such as diaries or PDAs, useful. To-do lists and calendars suit your personality type because they provide the flexibility you need to multi-task effectively. You get your energy from active involvement in things and with people, so it's important to schedule meetings accordingly.

Make sure that you have thought things through before embarking on a project or attending a meeting. Extraverts have a tendency to jump into action because this is what they derive their energy from.

Introvert

If you tend to be introverted and like to reflect before you act, plan your schedule so that you have time to think before working on difficult or creative tasks. This will allow you to think without distractions from others, and can help you use your time more effectively.

You may find broad overviews useful when planning your time because these help you to process what needs to be done internally before engaging with the world. Remember to get feedback from others when planning your time so you are aware of how their work may impact your schedule.

Sensor

If you are a sensor, it's important for you to define your tasks and goals in concrete terms in order to better manage your time. You may find planning on paper useful.

Because you tend to focus on the present, it's important that you remember long-term goals when planning your time. You also pay a lot of attention to facts, either past or present – so much so that you may miss new possibilities, which could slow down your work in the end. Remember to stand back from the facts sometimes. You may even want to schedule time for looking at the broader picture when you feel you are getting bogged down in concrete details.

Intuitive

If you have a preference for intuition, you can benefit by keeping a log of past events and work that you have completed. This will help you remember any important points for future work of a similar kind, thereby helping you complete it more effectively and quickly.

Because you like doing things that are new and different, you should schedule time for developing new ideas. This will help you shape those possibilities into reality over time. Creating a system for classifying your tasks and the relationships between them helps you to harness your flair for patterns. However, you need to check carefully to make sure that you have taken all factors into account.

Thinker

If you are a thinker, you may do well with systematized, or cyclical, schedules that can be established on a weekly or monthly basis, because such systems create consistency. Creating schedules helps to break tasks into their logical components, and it generates concrete deadlines and goals.

Thinkers make decisions that are rational, consistent, and goal-orientated. They can make the most of these traits when planning their time management. However, it's important to stay flexible. You may need to consider people, along with facts. It's a good idea to allow extra time in your schedule for accommodating unexpected changes and so that you can respond to other people's requirements.

Feeler

In situations where you need to make a decision, you may need to refocus and take a more objective position in order to get the decision made more quickly.

Judger

If you have a preference for judging, you like to have things organized and matters settled, and it's likely that you're pretty good at planning your time.

However, you also need to allow flexibility in your plans so that you can react to unforeseen circumstances and have time for unplanned tasks.

Perceiver

If you are a perceiver, you may need to plan carefully to stay focused and avoid being late. Your schedule should provide an overview of the big picture and of your priorities so that it matches your natural way of perceiving and dealing with the world.

Plan your time in blocks, rather than hour by hour, to allow for fluctuating energy levels and to remain flexible enough to respond to changing situations. Frequently reviewed to-do lists with clear deadlines suit your personality type better than tight schedules because they allow you to be flexible without losing sight of your priorities. Planning loosely around definite deadlines will help you to stay open to new information, while still making timely decisions and meeting your goals.

Question

Match time management guidelines to the personality types that would most benefit from them.

Options:

A. Develop flexible plans to react to unforeseen circumstances

Effective Time Management

B. Tighten up planning; set more deadlines to interest you

C. Focus on facts, not pleasing people; set clear priorities and deadlines in line with known rules and systems

D. Define tasks and goals in concrete terms

E. Plan your time so you work on several projects at once

F. Consult others before setting meeting times

Targets:
1. Judger
2. Perceiver
3. Feeler
4. Sensor
5. Extravert
6. Introvert

Answer:

Judgers have a strong drive to be in control, and this can make them inflexible and overly focused on procedures or following a set schedule.

Perceivers enjoy working to deadlines, but because they like to be able to react to changing situations rather than planning ahead, they may have to pay more attention to the need to plan their time.

Because feelers put so much energy into pleasing others and sometimes fail to be objective, they need to focus more on facts and ensure that they adhere to organizational protocols.

Sensors need to define tasks and goals in concrete terms to ensure that they are meaningful. They work well with schedules and deadlines, but need to make sure that they include long-term goals in their plans.

Extraverts thrive on plenty of stimulation, so working on several projects at once is useful. However, you may neglect to plan ahead.

Because introverts do so much of their thinking on their own, they may forget to get feedback from others to check their decisions.

CHAPTER II - PLANNING AND PRIORITIZING YOUR TIME

CHAPTER II - Planning and Prioritizing Your Time

Time management starts with you identifying your goals. When you know your goals, you can determine how much time you will need to achieve them. Goals are specific, desired outcomes you identify to assist you in determining what it is you need to do and when. Without goals, it's easy to spend time on tasks that have no clearly defined purpose.

A to-do list contains the tasks you need to complete in order to achieve your goals. It reminds you of what you need to accomplish.

Once you have your to-do list, you need to give each task a priority. To prioritize work effectively, you can use a priority matrix, which divides work into urgent and important categories. All of the tasks that are performed during your working day can be included under one of the headings in the priority matrix. This topic will look more closely at how tasks fit into these different quadrants of the priority matrix.

During the course of your business day, you need to manage your tasks in relation to the time available to you. The way you schedule most of your tasks will center around their deadlines and completion dates. However, some tasks may also have specific start dates or even dependencies that affect when you can schedule them.

For instance, the completion of one of your tasks may depend entirely on someone else completing another task. Or you may not be able to start work on your task until the necessary resources become available.

In the average business, many demands are placed on employees' time. It can sometimes be difficult to determine exactly what you need to do, when you need to start and complete a task, and precisely how long the task will take you to complete. You may have numerous tasks that require your attention and that compete for your time. So how do you decide what to do first?

When you're faced with what seems like an overwhelming workload, queuing may be your best option. This is a method in which you place tasks into a queue and then prioritize them.

To manage your time well, you should know not only what tasks you need to accomplish, but also when those tasks must be completed and how long they'll take. Making accurate estimates about how long a task will take is one of the keys to effective time management. Many management problems are the result of unrealistic estimates of how long it will take to complete specific tasks.

If you estimate time frames accurately, you'll be able to schedule your work more efficiently and ensure that you meet deadlines.

It's important to estimate the time frames for your tasks accurately so that you can schedule all your work effectively and meet deadlines. But how do you go about doing this?

First you need to know the requirements of each task, and your experience with activities – both when they run smoothly and when they don't – to produce three time estimates. These are likely time, shortest time, and longest time. These three elements work together to produce a realistic time estimate.

GOALS AS A TIME MANAGEMENT TOOL

Goals as a time management tool

Time management starts with you identifying your goals. When you know your goals, you can determine how much time you will need to achieve them. Goals are specific, desired outcomes you identify to assist you in determining what it is you need to do and when. Without goals, it's easy to spend time on tasks that have no clearly defined purpose.

Question

Which do you think is the best example of an effective goal?

Options:

1. Produce a sales report
2. Recruit three new staff members by August 31
3. Sales conference plans by October 31

Answer:

Effective goals have certain characteristics. They're typically specific, measurable, achievable, realistic, and time-related.

Option 1: This option is incorrect. Although this goal states what it is you wish to achieve, it's not specific, measurable, or time-related and therefore far too vague.

Option 2: This option is correct. This goal is specific and measurable – you know exactly how many staff you need to recruit and by when. It gives you a clear idea of what you're working toward and what your desired outcome is. Therefore, you can plan your time accordingly.

Option 3: This is an incorrect option. Although this goal is time-related, it's not specific enough and it's not phrased as an action. Effective goals are action-centered.

Effective goals have the characteristics represented by the mnemonic **SMART**:

- they are specific so you have a clear picture of what needs to be done,
- they are measurable in that they define specific criteria for measuring progress toward their accomplishment – for example, increase sales by 10%,
- they are attainable, in that they reflect your skills and abilities,
- they are realistic, taking into account your present circumstances, including your willingness and ability to,
- work toward the goal, and
- they are time-related, in that they include deadlines.

Specific goals are more useful than vague ones. For instance, it's not enough to state that you want to increase product sales.

Vague goals such as this one mean your results will be equally vague. You need to answer several questions, such as who, what, where, when, which, and why, when you write a goal.

Setting a goal to increase product sales by 25% in the next three months is a more specific and effective goal.

Goals should also be measurable, answering questions such as "How much?" "How many?" and "What percentage?" With the goal to increase product sales by 25% in the next three months, you can track and measure how far you are from the 25% increase along the way.

As well as being specific and measurable, goals should be attainable and realistic.

Is a goal to complete a comprehensive report in one week achievable, when you won't have all the information for that report until one day before it's due? Probably not. It's easier to attain your goals when you plan your steps wisely and establish a time frame that allows you to carry out those steps.

And what about setting a goal to obtain a law degree within two years when you have a full-time job and a family of four, including an elderly parent to care for? This isn't very realistic or practical. Goals should take into consideration both professional and personal factors.

Finally, goals should be time-related. You should set precise deadlines for achieving your goals and then create a schedule of all the tasks that are necessary to meet your deadlines. It can help to create a to-do list, outlining all those tasks. For example, if you need to complete a financial report by the end of the month, you might list "get sales figures from managers" as one task.

ATTRIBUTES OF A GOOD TO-DO LIST

Attributes of a good to-do list

A to-do list contains the tasks you need to complete in order to achieve your goals. It reminds you of what you need to accomplish.

Andrea, who works in the HR Department of a large commercial bank, has two main goals that she needs to focus on. First, she has to publish an advertisement for three job roles that will become vacant within the next four months. Second, she must send a letter to the ten unsuccessful candidates for a marketing position by the end of next week.

Each of these goals has certain associated activities, and Andrea has created a to-do list to help her achieve them.

Andrea's to-do list is divided up into two main goals. Each goal is broken down into specific activities. The first goal is to publish an advertisement for the three vacant job roles that will exist within the next four months, and the second goal is to send a letter to the ten unsuccessful candidates for the marketing position by the end of next week. The activities that fall under the first goal are to contact the newspaper and arrange publication dates, agree on the size and cost of an advertisement, and write a short paragraph describing each job role. The activities that fall under the second goal are to decide on the content of the letter, type the letters to each of the candidates, send the letters out and keep copies in the company file, and send copies of the letters to Theresa in Marketing.

Because Andrea has identified what her two main goals are, she has been able to break these down into individual tasks. Her to-do list includes a short-term goal and a long-term goal.

See each type of goal to learn more about it.

Short-term goal

A short-term goal is sometimes referred to as an enabling goal because it can help you achieve a long-term goal. It can be viewed as a stepping stone that enables you to measure your progress in achieving your longer-term goals. A short-term goal is also a goal that is generally achieved in the near future.

In Andrea's case, her short-term goal is to send letters to the ten unsuccessful candidates for the marketing position. This is a short-term goal because it needs to be achieved by the end of the week.

Long-term goal

A long-term goal is a goal that is achieved over a longer period of time – for instance, a few months or even years.

Andrea's first goal – publishing an advertisement for the three vacant job roles – is an example of a long-term goal. This is because she has four months within which to achieve it.

Effective Time Management

Like goals, the items on your to-do list should meet certain criteria. You can remember the four criteria you should apply using the mnemonic AIMS:

- they should be action-centered, pinpointing specific actions that are required for you to meet your goals,
- they should be incremental, breaking actions into smaller, more manageable activities,
- they should be measurable, including criteria you'll use to measure whether each task has been completed successfully – for example, an item on a to-do list might be to process two customer orders, and
- they should be scheduled realistically, based on the time frame within which you expect to complete them – working according to a schedule increases the probability that you'll complete each task.

Suppose your goal is to plan a November sales conference by mid-September. One of the tasks you've listed for this goal is "upcoming sales conference arrangements." This is not action-centered, and it's not very clear what needs to be done. To make this more effective, you need to break the task down and use action verbs. For example, you might list "book a venue for the conference by July 1," "acquire ten speakers by July 15," "create the program schedule by September 15," and "prepare the opening presentation" as the required tasks.

When you have tasks or goals that are large, such as making arrangements for a sales conference, it can help to define and isolate the components of those tasks.

Then you'll understand what steps are involved and in what order they should be completed in order to achieve the larger goal.

Be sure the tasks on your list are also measurable. For example, the task "prepare opening presentation for the conference" is not measurable.

But if you rewrite this as "prepare a 20-minute opening presentation on e-books," it becomes a measurable task.

Use of words like "all," "current," and "relevant" give clues as to how to measure the completion of a task. For example, a task like "find the most recent information on e-books" is specific about what information must be found. Remember, the more specific you are, the easier it is to measure your success in finishing the task.

You can schedule the task by adding a timeframe to it – for example, "prepare a 20-minute presentation on e-books by October 26."

It's important that you don't put too many tasks on your list. Being realistic in your expectations and your time estimates is key. Consider the tasks that absolutely require your attention – tasks that no one else can do, for example – and put those on your list. But remember, too, to keep things in perspective. Don't think of your to-do list as a list of commands, but rather of possibilities.

Question

Tom has created a to-do list identifying tasks for his goal of preparing a presentation on his company's new product design.

Which AIMS criteria has Tom successfully incorporated into his to-do list?

Tom's to-do list is made up of five tasks. Task one is to create two key objectives for the presentation. Task two is

Effective Time Management

to research the latest information regarding the new product design. The third task is to write the relevant content for the presentation. The fourth task is to design all the presentation slides, and the fifth task is to create notes from the presentation slides and print 25 sets of notes for the presentation attendees.

Options:
1. Action-centered
2. Incremental
3. Scheduled
4. Measurable

Answer:

Option 1: This is a correct option. Tom's to-do list is action-centered because it consists of tasks he needs to perform in order to realize the goal of producing and delivering a good presentation. Notice how each of Tom's tasks begins with an action verb, which emphasizes the "doing" part of the task.

Option 2: This option is correct. Tom has broken down the larger goal or task of preparing a presentation into several smaller, incremental tasks. Tasks can be discouraging unless you break them down into more manageable activities.

Option 3: This is an incorrect option. Although Tom's to-do list incorporates all other points of the AIMS criteria, his list isn't scheduled. Tom didn't structure his tasks around a schedule, nor did he indicate approximate times for each activity.

Option 4: This option is correct. The tasks on Tom's list are measurable – for example, the tasks described as "create two key objectives" and "print 25 sets of notes" include specific information about how many objectives and sets of notes are required. In addition, his use of such words as "latest," "relevant," and "all" indicates possible ways to measure the completion of the tasks.

THE PRIORITY MATRIX

The priority matrix
Once you have your to-do list, you need to give each task a priority. To prioritize work effectively, you can use a priority matrix, which divides work into urgent and important categories. All of the tasks that are performed during your working day can be included under one of the headings in the priority matrix. This topic will look more closely at how tasks fit into these different quadrants of the priority matrix.

The priority matrix is divided into four quadrants. The top left quadrant represents urgent and important tasks. The top right quadrant represents tasks that are important but not urgent. The bottom left quadrant represents tasks that are urgent but not important, and the bottom right quadrant represents tasks that are not urgent and not important.

Urgent tasks tend to be those that demand immediate attention, are highly visible, and are of importance to others. They may be attractive to you because working on them makes you feel that you're achieving something quickly.

Important tasks, on the other hand, are those that help you achieve your long-term mission or goals. They require more planning. To respond to important tasks, you can't just be reactive – you have to be proactive.

A priority matrix helps you distinguish between tasks that are urgent and important, those that are important but not urgent, those that are urgent but not important, and finally, those that are not urgent and not important.

See each area in the priority matrix to find out where different tasks fit in.

Important and urgent tasks

Important and urgent tasks have the highest priority and should be dealt with first. You should devote as much time and effort to them as possible.

Tasks in this quadrant include emergencies, deadline-driven projects, or problems that require immediate action.

Important but not urgent

Tasks that are important but not urgent include planning, relationship building, networking, personal development, or identifying new opportunities.

These are often the preferred tasks – the ones you would like to do first because they tend to be more interesting.

Don't ignore these tasks, but try to put some time aside each day to work on them. If they are left too long, they can become urgent.

Urgent but not important

Tasks that are urgent but not important include interruptions, some phone calls, e-mails, and meetings, and requests to help out another person.

Because these tasks are not important, you don't want to lose too much time on them. They may be urgent but they are not important to you personally, so deal with them as quickly as you can and move on.

Not urgent and not important

Tasks that are neither important nor urgent may include, for example, surfing the web with no particular goal in mind, or chatting to colleagues about last night's sports results.

These tasks have the lowest priority. Complete these tasks only when you have nothing more important to do.

Question

Match each priority matrix category to a description of the types of tasks it should contain.

Options:

A. Urgent but not important
B. Not urgent and not important
C. Urgent and important
D. Important but not urgent

Targets:

1. Tasks such as these should be addressed promptly but you shouldn't spend too much time on them
2. These tasks have the lowest priority and can be completed when other tasks are done
3. Tasks in this category should be completed as soon as possible; they have the highest priority
4. Tasks in this category include networking and relationship building, and are often the preferred tasks because they tend to be more interesting

Answer:

These tasks are urgent, so you need to deal with them. However, you shouldn't spend too much time on them. Although they may be urgent, they're not important to you personally, so deal with them as quickly as possible and move on.

You can attend to tasks that are not urgent or important when you have nothing more important to do.

Tasks that are urgent and important require your full attention and should be completed first. You should devote as much time and effort to these types of tasks as you can.

Tasks that are important but not urgent, like networking or relationship building, tend to be more interesting and therefore ones you'd prefer doing. It's best to try to set some time aside each day to work on them. If they're left too long, these tasks can become urgent.

Once you know what tasks you have to perform, you can use the priority matrix to determine the level of importance of each one.

Consider the to-do list of Candy, who is the administrative assistant to Michael, the president of a large shipping company.

The tasks in Candy's to-do list are as follows:

Task 1, type up Michael's presentation notes for the senior management meeting tomorrow.

Task 2, answer a coworker's telephone while she is at lunch.

Task 3, reserve a hotel room for Michael's trip to Australia next quarter.

Task 4, source a company to provide some more exotic flower arrangements for the reception area.

Effective Time Management

Task 5, order lunch for tomorrow's senior management meeting.

Task 6, deal with Deal with interruptions from colleagues asking about Michael's availability.

Task 7, put together a new filing system for Michael's financial reports.

Task 8, look at Michael's vacation photographs.

Candy needs to use the priority matrix to determine the level of importance of each task. This will have an effect on the order in which she completes all the tasks.

You could, of course, review each quadrant of the priority matrix to find out how Candy categorizes each of the tasks from her to-do list.

Important and urgent tasks

Candy identifies typing up Michael's presentation notes for the senior management meeting the next day and ordering lunch for that meeting as important and urgent tasks.

Important but not urgent

Important tasks that are not urgent are reserving a hotel room for Michael's trip to Australia next quarter and putting together a new filing system for Michael's financial reports.

Urgent but not important

Urgent but not important tasks are answering a coworker's telephone while she is at lunch and dealing with interruptions from colleagues asking about Michael's availability.

Not urgent and not important

Tasks that are neither urgent nor important in Candy's to-do list are looking at Michael's vacation photographs and sourcing a company to provide some more exotic flower arrangements for the reception area.

Question

Match the tasks to the appropriate quadrants on the priority matrix.

The priority matrix is divided into four quadrants. The first quadrant represents urgent and important tasks. The second quadrant represents tasks that are important but not urgent. The third quadrant represents tasks that are urgent but not important, and the fourth quadrant represents tasks that are not urgent and not important.

Options:

A. Fix a problem with the server that is causing work delays

B. Set up a username and password for a new employee who's due to start in two months

C. Address an interruption from a colleague about system software

D. Read through brochures about a conference next year

Targets:

1. In the priority matrix, the first quadrant is for tasks that are urgent and important.

2. In the priority matrix, the second quadrant is for tasks that are important but not urgent.

3. In the priority matrix, the third quadrant is for tasks that are urgent but not important.

4. In the priority matrix, the fourth quadrant is for tasks that are neither urgent nor important.

Answer:

Effective Time Management

Fixing a fault on the server is an urgent task that's also important. It requires immediate action because employee productivity will be affected if it's not done.

Although setting up a username and password is important, it's not urgent because you still have two months to complete this task.

Although dealing with an interruption is urgent, it's not important. The task is urgent because you must do it immediately, but it's not important because it may not be part of your regular work.

Reading through brochures for a conference scheduled for next year isn't important and isn't urgent. It's in no way time-critical, no other tasks depend on it, and nobody else is negatively affected if you don't get to it.

Once you've prioritized your tasks, the next step is to schedule your tasks. To do this, you set aside specific times for their completion to ensure each one will get done.

SEQUENCING

Sequencing
During the course of your business day, you need to manage your tasks in relation to the time available to you. The way you schedule most of your tasks will center around their deadlines and completion dates. However, some tasks may also have specific start dates or even dependencies that affect when you can schedule them.

For instance, the completion of one of your tasks may depend entirely on someone else completing another task. Or you may not be able to start work on your task until the necessary resources become available.

This is where the concept of sequencing can be helpfully applied.

Sequencing is a process in which you plan your time by taking start dates into account.

It allows you to quickly review what you need to do and whether there is time available to complete the required tasks.

Sequencing is most effective when you have large tasks that need to be completed and when you're aware, in advance, of what needs to be done.

To sequence your tasks effectively, you follow three steps – distinguish between sequential and parallel tasks, schedule tasks, and, where necessary, renegotiate deadlines.

Sequential tasks can't start until other tasks have been completed. For instance, you can start writing a financial report on three departments only once those departments supply you with the relevant financial figures.

So dependent tasks need to be completed in a sequence, with each task being more or less finished before the next task can begin. A simple example is constructing a house – you can't start building the inner walls until the foundation and outer structure are complete.

Parallel tasks, on the other hand, are not dependent on any other factors for their start dates. They may be done at any time before or after a particular stage is reached. For example, writing a review of a book in your field is something that is not dependent on other factors for its start date.

Whether a task is parallel or sequential depends largely on its context.

Some questions you might ask when distinguishing between tasks are: When can you start and what's the deadline? Is the task dependent on someone else finishing something first and do you need anything before you can start? How long will the task take?

Question

Which do you think is the best way to start scheduling your sequential and parallel tasks?

Options:

1. Schedule the sequential tasks by their earliest start dates
2. Start with parallel tasks and work the sequential tasks around them
3. Schedule the sequential task that's most difficult first

Answer:

Option 1: This is the correct option. You determine the earliest start dates for sequential tasks based on the availability of resources or the completion dates of other tasks on which the sequential tasks depend. Scheduling sequential tasks first will help you get a clearer picture of how realistic your schedule is.

Option 2: This option is incorrect. You should schedule sequential tasks first because they're dependent on other factors. Then you can fit in parallel tasks around those.

Option 3: This is an incorrect option. You need to analyze start and completion dates – rather than levels of difficulty – to schedule tasks effectively.

To schedule your tasks, you start with the sequential tasks, scheduling the earliest start dates of each of these. You determine each start date based on the availability of resources or on the completion date for another task on which the sequential task depends. You then schedule your parallel tasks to fall into the time gaps that exist between the sequential tasks.

For instance, you've received two of the three departmental financial statements that you need to collate into a financial report.

While you're waiting for the remaining one, you can fit in the parallel task of making a list of resources you need for a staff leadership workshop you're planning.

Effective Time Management

Sometimes, the earliest start dates, time frames for completion, and deadlines are not compatible.

If you've assessed all your tasks and determined that some deadlines may not be achievable, you need to renegotiate these deadlines.

Remember, however, that if people are dependent on the completion of your tasks for the completion of theirs, it may not be possible to renegotiate deadlines. Generally, there's more room for renegotiation if your deadline is the final date for overall completion of specific work.

For example, you realize that one of three outstanding departmental statements you require to complete a financial report will not be ready in time to meet your final deadline.

You can probably renegotiate the deadline for your submission of the full financial report because you are at the end of the process.

Gloria is the marketing manager for a leading-edge software company. She has several tasks to complete this week.

She works eight hours each day, between 9:00 a.m. and 6:00 p.m., and takes lunch each day from 1:00 p.m. to 2:00 p.m. During this particular week, she has to have all tasks completed by 6:00 p.m. on Friday night.

Question

Gloria needs to distinguish between parallel and sequential tasks. Which statements do you think apply to the tasks outlined for her week?

Options:

1. Drafting and producing the information leaflets for the Marketing Dynamics conference is a parallel task

2. Finalizing the New York marketing seminar budget is a sequential task

3. Putting together an initial project plan for the Marketing Essentials conference is a parallel task

4. Creating marketing material for the blogging workshops is a parallel task

Answer:

Option 1: This option is incorrect. Task 1 is a sequential task because Gloria can only start it after she's received the relevant information from Lauren.

Option 2: This is a correct option. Task 3 is a sequential task because Gloria needs the relevant figures from Jermaine before she can start it.

Option 3: This option is correct. Task 2 is a parallel task because it doesn't depend on the completion of any other task or on the availability of any resources.

Option 4: This is an incorrect option. Gloria can only start task 4 after the venues have been confirmed, making this a sequential task.

The first step Gloria takes is to distinguish between sequential and parallel tasks.

The tasks in Gloria's to-do list are as follows:

Task 1, drafting and producing information leaflets for the Marketing Dynamics conference in Los Angeles is a sequential task.

Task 2, putting together an initial project plan for the Marketing Essentials conference is a parallel task.

Task 3, finalizing the budget for the New York marketing seminar is a sequential task.

Task 4, producing marketing plans for the next six international blogging workshops is a sequential task.

She knows that tasks 1, 3, and 4 are sequential because they depend on other factors for their start dates. Task 2 is parallel because Gloria doesn't have to wait for anything before starting it.

She now has to schedule her tasks appropriately to ensure they're all completed. She does this by reviewing the start dates and deadlines of all the sequential tasks.

Question

Which statements best describe how Gloria should schedule her tasks?

Options:

1. Gloria should schedule task 1 to start Monday at 2:00 p.m. when the information she needs becomes available

2. Task 3 should be scheduled for first thing on Monday morning

3. Task 4 should be scheduled for Friday

4. Task 2 can be slotted in on Monday morning before starting any sequential tasks

Answer:

Option 1: This option is correct. Gloria can't start task 1 until Monday at 2:00 p.m. when she's due to receive the information she needs from Lauren.

Option 2: This is an incorrect option. The figures Gloria needs for task 3 won't be ready until Tuesday morning, so she shouldn't schedule this task to start on Monday.

Option 3: This is a correct option. Gloria will need to complete task 4 by the end of the week because the design team will need marketing plans by the following Monday.

Option 4: This option is correct. Task 2 is a parallel task that can fit in around the sequential tasks. Gloria won't be able to start any sequential tasks until 2:00 p.m. on Monday, so she can work on task 2 Monday morning.

After reviewing her tasks, Gloria schedules them. Task 1 can get under way only at 2:00 p.m. on Monday.

On Wednesday morning, she can work on task 3, which requires 18 working hours. Task 4, which takes 6 hours, needs to be finished by the end of Friday.

Question

Gloria now needs to determine whether she needs to renegotiate any deadlines. Which deadlines, if any, should Gloria renegotiate?

Options:

1. None
2. Task 1
3. Task 2
4. Task 4
5. Task 3

Answer:

Option 1: This is the correct option. Gloria doesn't need to renegotiate any deadlines. She's able to accommodate all tasks into her work schedule.

Option 2: This option is incorrect. Three departments are relying on the completion of task 1 to commence their activities, so renegotiating the deadline for this task wouldn't be easy.

Option 3: This option is incorrect. Task 2 is a parallel task and therefore doesn't need to be renegotiated. Gloria can fit this task around her sequential tasks.

Option 4: This option is incorrect. Two departments are relying on the completion of task 4 to commence their activities, so Gloria probably won't be able to renegotiate the deadline for this task.

Option 5: This option is incorrect. Gloria will complete task 3 on Friday morning and move on to complete task 4 before the end of the day.

To sequence her tasks effectively, Gloria first distinguished between them. She categorized tasks 1, 3, and 4 as sequential and task 2 as parallel.

Gloria looked at the earliest possible start date and worked from there to schedule her tasks according to deadlines and other start dates.

In the end, she was able to schedule her tasks so that she completed them by Friday afternoon. This meant that she did not need to renegotiate any deadlines.

QUEUING

Queuing

In the average business, many demands are placed on employees' time. It can sometimes be difficult to determine exactly what you need to do, when you need to start and complete a task, and precisely how long the task will take you to complete. You may have numerous tasks that require your attention and that compete for your time. So how do you decide what to do first?

When you're faced with what seems like an overwhelming workload, queuing may be your best option. This is a method in which you place tasks into a queue and then prioritize them.

You can prioritize tasks in a queue in several ways – by place in line, customer status, processing time, or due date.

See each queuing method for prioritizing tasks to learn more about it.

Place in line

Dealing with tasks by using the place in line method simply means that you deal with your tasks on a "first come, first served" basis.

Customer status

Using the customer status method means you consider the requirements or needs of the person who's making the request and then respond to the most urgent requirements or needs first.

Processing time

The processing time method involves completing the easiest and quickest jobs first, because they have the shortest processing times. By doing this, you clear a large amount of tasks in a short period of time.

Due date

Using the due date method, you process tasks based solely on their due dates. As such, the task with the closest deadline will be completed first.

Queuing is most effective as a way to manage your time when you have to juggle conflicting deadlines. If you have time to plan effectively, you probably won't need to use queuing at all.

But if you do decide to use queuing, you should consider the pros and cons of each method.

The method you choose should depend on your specific circumstances and the industry in which you work.

See each queuing method to review the associated pros and cons.

Place in line

Because the place in line method simply involves dealing with tasks on a "first come, first served" basis, it's the easiest to administer and seems fair. However, it may lead to inefficiency because it requires that you move quickly between dissimilar tasks.

This method is practical in a customer-facing environment. For instance, in the case of a restaurant where customers queue to be seated, it's best to use the place in line method. That way customers are seated according to the order in which they arrived at the restaurant.

Customer status

The customer status method is useful in a health or social care environment. But it does involve you in detailed assessments of customer needs.

In other industries, such as the restaurant business, this status-driven approach could be viewed as "ranking customers" and so lead to conflict.

Processing time

Queuing tasks according to their processing times may give you the immediate satisfaction of completing several short tasks. It's most effective when you have lots of routine tasks to perform.

However, you may find that you're not making effective use of your available time by focusing on the easiest tasks. It could be that you're putting off more important tasks.

Due date

Working according to the closest deadline or due date is a reactive method. You're simply "fire fighting" and creating a cycle in which deadlines move ever closer.

This method works best if you have fixed deadlines – for instance, in logistics.

Four individuals, each working in a different industry, use different queuing methods. They use queuing to help them deal with their different types of workloads.

See each of the four individuals to find out more about the queuing methods they use.

Tina

Tina works as a receptionist in the emergency unit of a hospital. The emergency unit is always busy and, although most patients demand to see a doctor right away, Tina has first to assess the specific needs of each patient. She can't refer patients to doctors on a first come, first served basis because certain patient injuries are more life-threatening than others.

As such, Tina makes use of the customer status method to prioritize and manage all patients who come into the emergency room.

Sally

Sally manages a very busy, upmarket clothing store. Every day, she deals with customers who have questions regarding sizing, fabric care, styling, and new ranges of clothing. She doesn't have an assistant, so at times, customer demands can be overwhelming.

For this reason, Sally deals with customer queries using the place in line method. This way, customers are served on a fair, first come, first served basis.

Adam

Adam works as a help desk agent for an Internet service provider. He provides support via e-mail to customers who are experiencing difficulties with the service provider.

His company assures all clients with quick and quality service. So Adam prioritizes all his queries according to their processing times. He deals with problems that are the quickest to resolve first.

Ted

Ted works for a busy radio station. He's a senior producer, which means he must make sure that several programs make it to air on time each week. He works with very strict deadlines. As a result, he queues his work on the basis of earliest deadline first.

He gives priority to the programs that have the nearest deadlines, although he has other programs to work on. So those programs that come later in the week are put back in the queue.

Tina, Sally, Adam, and Ted use the most effective queuing methods for their circumstances.

Tina's circumstance within the health care environment requires her to use the customer status method, whereas Sally's customer-facing environment in the clothing store is well suited to the place in line method.

Adam's best approach to dealing with his client queries as quickly as possible is to process the quickest tasks first. So he uses the processing time method. Ted, on the other hand, uses the due date method to queue his work because all his tasks have very specific deadlines.

Question

Match each queuing method to the circumstance in which its use is most appropriate.

Options:

A. Place in line
B. Due date
C. Processing time
D. Customer status

Targets:

1. Jennifer, an information officer at a university, must address many students in person throughout her day, answering various questions from them

Effective Time Management

2. Lucille creates itineraries and makes bookings for travelers, and she sometimes has clients who give very short notice of their travel plans

3. Ted processes routine insurance claims, some of which take longer than others to process 4. Jeremy provides trauma counseling to walk-in patients at a busy hospital

Answer:

Jennifer should use the place in line method when meeting with students face-to-face. With this method, she'll address students on a first come, first served basis, which is fair for everyone.

Lucille should make use of the due date method of queuing because she needs to consider deadlines. Some customers want to leave on vacation with short notice – and she'll need to react to those more promptly.

The best queuing method for Ted is prioritizing his claims by processing time. In this way, he can process the simplest claims first and then move on to those that are more complex and require more time to complete.

The best approach for Jeremy to use when queuing his work is to deal with patients on a customer status basis. This means that he'll tend to patients in the order indicated by an assessment of their needs. If someone is particularly stressed, he may need to put them at the front of the queue.

ESTIMATING TIME FRAMES

Estimating time frames

To manage your time well, you should know not only what tasks you need to accomplish, but also when those tasks must be completed and how long they'll take. Making accurate estimates about how long a task will take is one of the keys to effective time management. Many management problems are the result of unrealistic estimates of how long it will take to complete specific tasks.

If you estimate time frames accurately, you'll be able to schedule your work more efficiently and ensure that you meet deadlines.

See each way in which you can benefit from accurately estimating the time frames for your tasks to find out more about it.

Schedule work efficiently

Accurate estimates about how long tasks will take to complete make scheduling a lot easier. They ensure that you won't have to keep changing your schedule.

If you have a task that you accurately estimate will take six hours, for example, you can allot that time in your schedule and be reasonably confident you won't have to change the schedule.

But what if you didn't accurately estimate the time for that task and allotted it only three hours? It would throw your schedule off, and you'd need to rework it.

Meet deadlines

If you're accurate in estimating the time it will take to complete tasks, you'll be better able to meet your deadlines. If your estimates aren't accurate, you may need to ask to change deadlines or disappoint others who are relying on you to complete certain tasks.

With accurate time estimates, you'll also be more confident about setting deadlines because you know that the time you assign for completing each of your tasks is realistic.

Question

What are the benefits of accurately estimating time frames?

Options:

1. Helps you schedule your work more efficiently
2. Helps you create optimistic deadlines
3. Enables you to meet deadlines
4. Ensures that you will not run into any difficulties with your tasks

Answer:

Option 1: This option is correct. Accurate estimates about how long tasks will take to complete make scheduling easier. You won't have to keep changing your schedule because a task takes longer or shorter than expected. So estimating time frames accurately gives you a solid foundation for building a schedule.

Option 2: This is an incorrect option. Creating accurate estimates of how long tasks will take to complete helps you create deadlines that are realistic – rather than optimistic.

Option 3: This is a correct option. When you accurately estimate the time it takes to complete tasks, you'll be better able to meet your deadlines. If you didn't accurately estimate times, you'd likely need to ask to change deadlines. For example, if you assigned a task three hours when it really requires six, you could throw off your entire schedule and fall behind in your work, possibly missing deadlines.

Option 4: This option is incorrect. Although accurate estimates of how long tasks will take are important for scheduling purposes, they can't prevent unforeseen difficulties from arising and having to be dealt with.

TIME ESTIMATE EQUATION

Time estimate equation

It's important to estimate the time frames for your tasks accurately so that you can schedule all your work effectively and meet deadlines. But how do you go about doing this?

First you need to know the requirements of each task, and your experience with activities – both when they run smoothly and when they don't – to produce three time estimates. These are likely time, shortest time, and longest time. These three elements work together to produce a realistic time estimate.

See each element to learn more about it.

Likely time

The likely time is the time that the task normally takes you to complete.

It helps to consider the time it takes to complete the task without interruption. You should also think about a time frame you would be comfortable with based on your workload, the task, and any external factors that may delay or speed up the completion of the task.

Shortest time

The shortest time is the least amount of time that you have taken to complete the task in the past.

It may also refer to the shortest time in which you think you can complete the task if there are no interruptions or distractions.

Longest time

You can estimate the longest time by considering what may go wrong when performing the task and then adding this extra time to the task's likely duration.

This estimate should be based on your experience of this type of activity in the past, as well as on any foreseeable difficulties.

Question

Match each time frame with its corresponding description.

Options:

A. Likely time
B. Shortest time
C. Longest time

Targets:

1. The time frame that you're most comfortable with, considering your past experience with the task
2. The best time frame you can achieve, when everything runs smoothly
3. The time frame that takes into account everything that could go wrong while you're doing the task

Answer:

The likely time frame is the time it usually takes to complete the task, including the normal time involved in handling any interruptions and problems.

The shortest time refers to the fastest time a task will take to complete if you don't have any interruptions or problems.

The longest time frame takes into consideration problems that may crop up while you're completing the task. It's usually based on your experience of certain difficulties with the same type of task in the past.

You use the three time estimates to calculate the shortest possible time to complete a task based on an average of the likely, shortest, and longest times.

Because in most cases a task will take the likely time to complete, this time is given more weight. You need to multiply it by 4, add the shortest time, and then add the longest time. You divide the total by 6 to get the shortest possible time.

One important thing to remember is that you must use the same measurements for each type of time. For example, if your likely time is a number of days, the shortest and longest times must also be in days. If your estimates are in different measurements, start by changing them so they are all the same.

Now follow along to find out how to use the equation.

Figures for equation: First you need figures for the likely time, shortest time, and longest time estimates. In this case, the figures are 2 hours for the likely time, 30 minutes for the shortest time, and 4.5 hours for the longest time.

Same measurements: But you need to convert your estimates to the same measurements. Doing this gives you 120 minutes, 30 minutes, and 270 minutes.

Likely time: Next you multiply the likely time of 120 minutes by 4. This results in a figure of 480 minutes. To this value, you add the other two estimates – 30 minutes and 270 minutes.

Addition: You add up the figures in the numerator and come up with 780 minutes.

Division: Finally, you divide 780 minutes by 6. The result is 130 minutes.

Shortest possible time: So the shortest possible time for completing the task is 130 minutes, or 2 hours and 10 minutes.

Question

Sequence the steps for calculating the shortest possible completion time for a task.

Options:

A. Put times in the same format
B. Multiply the likely time estimate by 4
C. Add the times
D. Divide by 6

Answer:

Put times in the same format is ranked

The first step is to ensure that all times are in the same format. This is important for the equation to work properly.

Multiply the likely time estimate by 4 is ranked

The second step in the equation is to multiply the likely time by 4. The likely time estimate is given more weight in the equation because in most cases, the task will take this time to finish.

Add the times is ranked

The third step is to add the result of multiplying the likely time by 4 to the shortest and the longest times.

Effective Time Management

The time frames equation often produces a shortest possible time that is longer than the shortest time you put into the equation.

Divide by 6 is ranked

The last step in calculating the shortest possible time is to divide the result of adding the times by 6.

The time frames equation often produces a shortest possible time that is longer than the shortest time you put into the equation. This is because the equation helps ensure that you're realistic about how long things will take.

Question

Jonathan must estimate the shortest possible time it will take to collate and record the information from 50 customer feedback forms. He reviews previous performance records and estimates his times as follows: shortest time, 90 minutes; likely time, 120 minutes; and longest time, 3 hours.

What is the shortest possible time for completing the task, according to the time frames equation? You can access the job aid Using the Time Frames Equation to help answer this question.

Options:

1. 95 minutes
2. 125 minutes
3. 750 minutes

Answer:

Option 1: This option is incorrect. The likely time multiplied by 4 is 480 minutes. When the shortest and longest times are added, and the result divided by 6, the shortest possible time is 125 minutes. If you got 95 minutes, you likely didn't convert 3 hours to minutes.

Option 2: This is the correct option. The likely time multiplied by 4 is 480 minutes. When the shortest and longest times are added to this and divided by 6, the resulting figure, which is the shortest possible time, is 125 minutes.

Option 3: This is an incorrect option. Multiplying the likely time by 4 and adding the shortest time produces 570 minutes. When the longest time is added to this, the result is 750 minutes. However, this figure still has to be divided by 6, which produces the shortest possible time of 125 minutes.

CHAPTER III - AVOIDING TIME STEALERS

CHAPTER III - Avoiding Time Stealers

You need to produce a lengthy report, and it's time to get started. You create a new document. But your desk is untidy, so you spend a few minutes straightening it up. Then you quickly check for new e-mail messages and make coffee. Next you decide to reorganize the files containing the data you'll need to reference. Three hours later, you still haven't started work on the report.

So how can you overcome a habit of procrastination? Several strategies can help. These include considering the consequences of procrastinating, removing any obstacles causing you to delay a task, setting yourself a deadline, and simply taking the plunge and making a start somewhere.

Taking on too much work can have several negative consequences, both in your professional and home life:

- it can cause a high degree of stress and eventually lead you to "burn out",

- it can lead to neglect in your personal life, with overtime eating into time you'd spend with family and friends, relaxing, or exercising, and
- it can result in a failure to meet your core work responsibilities because you're too busy with other tasks.

Once you know your key goals and responsibilities, as well as how full your schedule is, you'll know how to respond when someone asks you to take on more work.

Saying "no" can be difficult, especially if it's your manager who asks you to take on a new responsibility. Even if it's a colleague who asks for your help when you're too busy to give it, it can be difficult to let go of the desire to please everyone.

However, remember that it can be much worse to take on a commitment you won't be able to meet than to say "no" in the first place.

You've blocked off exactly two hours to create an accounting spreadsheet. Next, a colleague comes to ask your advice about a software error. Your phone rings and it's an important client on the other end. And you notice that an e-mail marked urgent has arrived in your inbox.

For most people, an important part of work life is interacting with others. Breaks and socializing with colleagues are important too – sometimes you need time away from your desk.

But have you ever considered how much time you spend handling interruptions?

As a manager, Nina has an open-door policy. She knows it's important that her staff can come to her with any problems. In practice though, Nina spends so much time dealing with drop-in visitors that she's struggling to get her own work done.

Drop-in visitors are people who come into your office or to see you at your desk without a prior appointment. They can include managers, coworkers, customers or vendors, and friends.

Sometimes drop-in visitors want your help with problems or to discuss work-related issues. At other times, they may stop by just to chat. They can use up some of your valuable time.

BENEFITS OF OVERCOMING PROCRASTINATION

Benefits of overcoming procrastination

You need to produce a lengthy report, and it's time to get started. You create a new document. But your desk is untidy, so you spend a few minutes straightening it up. Then you quickly check for new e-mail messages and make coffee. Next you decide to reorganize the files containing the data you'll need to reference. Three hours later, you still haven't started work on the report.

Does any of this sound familiar? Do you put off what you can or should do now? This is called procrastinating.

Procrastinating often has negative consequences. Will you still be able to finish a long report in time if you really get going only at the eleventh hour? Even if you can, your work may not be up to scratch if it's rushed – and you're likely to feel guilty and stressed for as long as you put the work off.

Procrastination can sometimes be difficult to recognize. For example, if you have a deadline that's three months away, it can be easy to put off the work using the excuse that there's plenty of time.

But this is still a form of procrastination. And if you're saying the same thing a month later, chances are you may end up leaving the work so late that you can't finish it – or finish it well – by the deadline.

As the saying goes, "The surest way to be late is to have plenty of time."

See each of the common causes of procrastination for more information.

Not knowing where to start

If a task is complex or it's not clear what steps must be taken, you may delay taking any action at all. Spending too long considering all the alternatives or simply feeling overwhelmed can prevent you from getting down to work and determining what's actually required.

Avoiding unpleasant tasks

You may procrastinate out of a desire to avoid doing something uninteresting or unpleasant. For example, say you continually put off an important task like completing your tax forms. Instead of getting the job done, you spend your time on tasks that are less urgent but easier to complete and more interesting.

Being afraid of failure

Fear is a common and often unrecognized cause of procrastination. If you're faced with a task that's difficult, it may be your fear of failure that causes you to delay any action.

People who tend to be perfectionists don't want to produce work that's less than perfect, and this can paralyze them into not even making a start – sometimes until it's really too late to get a job done properly.

Overcoming a habit of procrastination can have several important benefits:
- you will be more productive – time that would otherwise be wasted will be spent on achieving results, and your work may be of a higher quality because you haven't had to rush it
- you will be less stressed, because you don't continually need to worry about work you know you should be doing and you won't feel the time pressures that procrastination can place on you, and finally
- you will have more control – by taking charge and not delaying action, you gain confidence in your ability to achieve goals and manage your own time

Question

Which are benefits of overcoming a habit of procrastination?

Options:

1. You'll avoid unpleasant or uninteresting tasks
2. You'll have a greater sense of control
3. You'll get more done
4. You'll have less work to do
5. You'll be less stressed

Answer:

Option 1: This is an incorrect option. Avoiding procrastination won't help you avoid unpleasant or tedious tasks, but it will help you get them out of the way – and often once you've made a start, a task proves easier than you might have imagined.

Option 2: This option is correct. Getting started on tasks as soon as you can will give you a greater sense of

Effective Time Management

control. You'll feel better able to get the work done and to manage your own time.

Option 3: This is a correct option. One of the main benefits of avoiding procrastination is that it makes you more productive. Delaying tactics waste time and prevent you from achieving results.

Option 4: This option is incorrect. Getting out of the habit of procrastinating won't actually reduce the amount of work you need to complete – but it can prevent the buildup of a stockpile of work that you've delayed doing.

Option 5: This option is correct. Avoiding procrastination eliminates the stress involved in knowing that you should be completing specific work but aren't, and that the time for doing this is running out.

BEATING PROCRASTINATION

Beating procrastination

So how can you overcome a habit of procrastination? Several strategies can help. These include considering the consequences of procrastinating, removing any obstacles causing you to delay a task, setting yourself a deadline, and simply taking the plunge and making a start somewhere.

If you're procrastinating, it can help get you going to consider what effects this may have. For example, you might identify these consequences:

- stress, which is likely to increase the longer you put off the work,
- having less time to complete work because of an initial delay, with the result that you may produce poor quality work,
- the possibility of missing a final deadline, and
- increased costs – this may apply if you have to pay for resources until a task is completed or if a financial penalty is associated with missing a deadline.

Effective Time Management

Sometimes it's necessary to put a task off. For example, you may need to put a task on hold until you've received the information or resources you need to complete it properly. This leads into another important strategy – identifying and removing any obstacles that are keeping you from making a start.

Even if obstacles such as lack of required information, resources, or equipment are easy to overcome, you may find yourself procrastinating.

For instance, you may need to make a phone call asking for particular information before you can start a job. Putting off the call also means putting off the task.

Other types of obstacles can get in your way too. For example, you may lack confidence about your ability to get a job done because you fear you don't have the necessary knowledge or skills.

If you've identified this as the reason why you're procrastinating, you can do something about it. Ask for or find the necessary help.

In this way, you remove the obstacles as a cause of procrastination.

Question

Tim has an audit report that's due next week. The client's files are in a mess, and Tim isn't sure how new tax legislation applies in the client's case. As a result, he's procrastinating about getting the work done.

Which are some of the ways that Tim can help himself stop procrastinating?

Options:

1. Focus on completing other, less urgent tasks in the meantime

2. Realize that he'll feel less stressed and do a better job if he stops delaying the work

3. Call the tax office to request information about how the new legislation must be applied

4. Request an extension so that more time for completing the audit is available

Answer:

Option 1: This is an incorrect option. Often, completing unimportant or low-priority tasks becomes an excuse for procrastinating about work that's more important.

Option 2: This option is correct. Identifying the consequences of procrastinating, such as stress and less time for completing the work properly once he starts, is likely to help motivate Tim to get the work done.

Option 3: This is a correct option. Once Tim has removed his lack of knowledge about the new legislation as an obstacle, it's likely to be easier for him to stop procrastinating.

Option 4: This option is incorrect. Tim will know if he needs additional time to complete the work only when he has made a proper start. Extending the deadline at this point may give him an excuse to continue procrastinating longer.

Another useful strategy is setting yourself a clear deadline for completing a task, and letting someone else know what this deadline is. In other words, make the deadline public. For example, you may tell a client you'll be ready to go over a proposal by a specific date, before you've actually written the proposal. You're more likely to stick to the deadline you've set if someone else is expecting you to do this.

Often getting started on a task is the hardest part of completing it.

So a good way to overcome procrastination is simply to jump in and do part of the work. There are many ways you might decide to do this.

If a job is complex and you don't know where to start, it can help to break it down into smaller tasks. Then place these in a logical sequence and simply start at the top of the list. Once you've completed the first task, it's likely you'll feel more confident about what's required and more motivated to continue.

And if it's fear that's holding you back, it can help to begin with the easiest task. Often, the best antidote for fear or indecision is taking action.

You may even want to get the most difficult or unpleasant task out of the way first.

This may require discipline, but it can also reduce stress. Once you've handled what's tricky or putting you off, you'll have a clear view toward the finish line.

An example can illustrate how to overcome procrastination. Natasha, a manager, has been putting off a meeting with an employee who has a consistently bad performance record. She has been procrastinating because she dislikes confrontation and fears the meeting may be a difficult one.

Consider how Natasha applies each of the strategies for overcoming procrastination. Review each strategy for more information.

Considering the consequences

Natasha considers the consequences of not taking action. For example, the employee's poor performance is likely to continue and to affect team morale. This helps motivate Natasha to stop procrastinating.

Removing obstacles

As a busy manager, Natasha is short on time. She identifies this as an obstacle that has been keeping her from meeting with the employee. So she makes a point of clearing two hours in her schedule for the next week by delegating an administrative task to someone she knows can handle it.

Setting a deadline

Natasha sets a date and time for meeting with the employee. Then she e-mails the employee a request to meet her at this time. Now she knows she'll have to follow through.

Making a start

Natasha begins work by finding all e-mail records documenting cases of poor performance by the employee. This is something simple for her to do – and once she has completed this task, she'll find it much easier to continue preparing for the meeting.

These additional guidelines can help you overcome a habit of procrastination:

- avoid being a perfectionist – although it's always good to do your best work, don't let impossibly high standards keep you from getting anything done at all,
- remember to prioritize tasks and don't use work that's not important – like organizing your e-mail or catching up on filing – as an excuse for postponing work that is, and

- schedule breaks or other types of rewards for once you've completed tasks or significant parts of the work that must be done.

Question

David has been asked to prepare a training manual for new software. He's missing information about the software's system requirements and isn't sure how best to structure the manual. As a result, he has been procrastinating about making a start for several days.

What can he do to overcome his procrastination?

Options:

1. Remember that if he continues to delay, he'll have less time to complete the manual and so will be under greater pressure

2. Complete other tasks until he feels confident about making a start on the manual

3. Begin by perfecting a structure for the manual

4. Start by writing a section of the manual that's straightforward and easy to complete

5. Let his manager know a date on which he plans to submit the manual

6. Ask the software developers for information about the software's system requirements

Answer:

Option 1: This option is correct. Considering the consequences of continuing to procrastinate can help motivate you to get a job done.

Option 2: This is an incorrect option. The longer David puts off making a start on the manual, the less time he'll have left to complete it and the more stressed he's likely to become.

Option 3: This option is incorrect. David will need to develop a structure for the manual. However, setting his standards too high could prevent him from getting the work done and encourage further procrastination.

Option 4: This is a correct option. Often starting by completing the easiest part of a task can help you overcome procrastination. It can give you a boost of confidence and momentum to continue with the work.

Option 5: This option is correct. Setting a deadline for completing a task and making this deadline public can help in overcoming procrastination.

Option 6: This is a correct option. David should identify and overcome any obstacles, such as missing information, that are keeping him from making a start.

HOW NOT TO TAKE ON TOO MUCH

How not to take on too much

Consider Mary, an employee who's always ready to volunteer for new assignments and to help others with theirs. Everyone knows that Mary is the person to turn to. The problem now is that she is working on three different projects at once. Although she works overtime, she just isn't managing to get everything done.

Are you anything like Mary? Do you tend to take on more work than you can realistically manage?

Taking on too much work can have several negative consequences, both in your professional and home life:

- it can cause a high degree of stress and eventually lead you to "burn out",
- it can lead to neglect in your personal life, with overtime eating into time you'd spend with family and friends, relaxing, or exercising, and
- it can result in a failure to meet your core work responsibilities because you're too busy with other tasks.

In addition to these negative consequences, taking on too much work often leads to multitasking. The problem with multitasking is that trying to do more than one thing at the same time often leads to mistakes. It's also generally inefficient and stressful. You just can't work as effectively if your concentration is scattered among several different jobs.

There are two main strategies for overcoming a tendency to take on too much work. The first is to know your key responsibilities and goals. And the second is to carefully plan how to use your time.

See each of the strategies for more information.

Know your key responsibilities

It's important to know what your key work responsibilities and goals are, so you can prioritize meeting these over taking on other assignments.

You should remind yourself that it isn't always possible to do everything. When you're feeling torn among different tasks, weigh up their relative importance in terms of your key goals. It can help to ask yourself the question, "What's the best or most important thing I could be doing now?"

Plan your time

You should plan your time carefully to ensure you spend it as productively as possible and that you don't take on more than you can manage.

This involves dividing your day into blocks of time and assigning an activity to each block. Activities you schedule might range from working on different tasks to managing your e-mail and making calls, to handling personal chores, and to getting enough rest.

Effective Time Management

You may also assign some flexible time, for unexpected tasks or those that take longer than planned to complete.

Once you've allocated all your available time and your schedule is full, you'll know you shouldn't make any more commitments.

As an editor in a publishing company, Martin has a schedule that's already hectic. However, other editors often turn to him for help with their manuscripts and managers often delegate administrative tasks to him.

He never says no, but the result is that despite working long hours, he sometimes misses his own deadlines.

Martin decides it's time to get more organized. He starts by identifying exactly what he needs to do, based on his job description and his goals. For instance, he needs to work on each of three manuscripts, which are at different stages in the editing cycle.

Martin's to-do list contains these tasks: Manuscript 1 – copyedit, Manuscript 2 - first edit, and Manuscript 3 - send letter to writer about changes.

Next, Martin buys a planner and assigns each of the tasks he knows he has to complete to a block of time in the day. He also schedules in the personal time he requires. For instance, he decides to ensure that he takes at least half an hour's break each lunchtime. This should help with concentration problems he's been having in the afternoons.

Martin's schedule is as follows: From 8:00 a.m. to 8:20 a.m., he handles e-mail. From 8:20 to 11:00 a.m., he edits chapter 7 of manuscript 1. From 11:00 a.m. to 12:00 p.m., he has a scheduled meeting with the writer of manuscript 2. From 12:00 p.m. to 1:30 p.m., he makes changes agreed with the writer and source graphics for manuscript 2. From 1:30 p.m. to 2:00 p.m., he takes a break. From 2:00 p.m. to 4:00 p.m., he checks the writer's implementation of edits for manuscript 3. From 4:00 p.m. to 5:00 p.m., he logs final edits for manuscript 3. From 5:00 p.m. to 5:45 p.m., he picks up his kids. From 5:45 p.m. to 8:00 p.m., he has supper and puts his kids to bed. From 8:00 p.m. to 8:30 p.m., he rests. And from 8:30 p.m. to 10:30 p.m., he spends time planning his family reunion.

By scheduling his time, it becomes clear to Martin what extra commitments he can or cannot fit in. In turn, this makes it easier for him to tell colleagues and managers when he doesn't have time to take on more work.

Question

Francesca is a busy legal secretary, but she can't seem to help saying yes when she's asked to pick up new work. As a result, she's often overtired and has started making mistakes.

In which ways can Francesca help overcome her tendency to take on too much work?

Options:

1. Plan for and request regular periods of leave
2. Weigh up the importance of each new assignment she's asked to accept in terms of her primary responsibilities and goals
3. Accept all assignments but ensure that she prioritizes them accurately based on their importance
4. Divide all her available time into blocks and distribute what she knows she has to get done among these blocks

Answer:

Option 1: This is an incorrect option. If Francesca continues taking on too much work, it's possible she'll

Effective Time Management

become so stressed that she'll have to request leave. But this won't help her in the long run. Instead, she needs to take steps to ensure her workload remains manageable.

Option 2: This is a correct option. Francesca should know her key work responsibilities and goals, and give these priority. If time is short, it's important that she doesn't take on other assignments that will compromise her ability to do what's really required of her.

Option 3: This option is incorrect. Sometimes it's not possible to do everything, irrespective of how well you plan your time. Francesca should prioritize key tasks, but she should also avoid taking on too much additional work.

Option 4: This option is correct. Scheduling her time carefully will help Francesca determine whether she's too busy to accept further assignments.

HOW TO SAY "NO"

How to say "no"
Once you know your key goals and responsibilities, as well as how full your schedule is, you'll know how to respond when someone asks you to take on more work.

Saying "no" can be difficult, especially if it's your manager who asks you to take on a new responsibility. Even if it's a colleague who asks for your help when you're too busy to give it, it can be difficult to let go of the desire to please everyone.

However, remember that it can be much worse to take on a commitment you won't be able to meet than to say "no" in the first place.

When you do say "no" to a request to take on more work, it's important to avoid causing offense or bad feeling. If it's your boss you need to say "no" to, it's also important to prevent your response from sounding like insubordination. This won't be good for your relationship – or your career.

So how can you say "no" without it having negative consequences? First, when appropriate, buy time before responding. Next, ensure that you say "no" in the right way. And finally, avoid inviting a discussion about why you're refusing the request.

See each of the strategies for more information.

Buy time

Particularly if it's your manager who asks you to take on more work, it's a good idea to say that you'd like some time to consider the request. Give your manager a deadline for when you will get back to him or her. This will give you time to determine whether your schedule really is too full and, if it is, to prepare a suitable response. It also shows that you're taking the request seriously. Simply returning an abrupt "no" would be disrespectful of your manager's authority.

When you buy time, it can also help to say that you appreciate having been asked to take on a particular responsibility. And remember, buying time doesn't mean changing the subject.

Say "no" in the right way

With either a manager or a colleague, it's always important to say "no" in a way that doesn't cause offense or appear unhelpful. Often the best approach is to make it clear how accepting more work will compromise your ability to meet your core responsibilities.

For example, make it clear why and how other important work will suffer if you have to spend time on something else.

Avoid a discussion

When you say "no," it's natural to want to justify your answer at some length. The problem with this approach is that too often, you may end up arguing yourself into a corner. For example, consider a statement like "I'm sorry,

I don't think I'm the right person for this." The other party may respond with an explanation of just why you are the right person for the job.

If you continue to argue at this point, you may be seen as uncooperative or plain difficult. The outcome could be that you agree to take on work you truly don't have the time to complete.

Scott works in advertising. He's currently busy on a campaign for an important client and is already struggling to fit everything he has to do into normal working hours.

Then, Scott's manager, Laura, asks him to create a portfolio to help secure a potential new contract. If the contract is signed, it will mean a steady stream of marketing work for the advertising agency over the next year.

Consider how Scott initially responds to his manager's request. Follow along with Scott and Laura's discussion.

Scott: It's wonderful that Gleeson Associates is considering giving us the work.

Laura: Yes, but first we need to win them over with a portfolio of some of the best work we've done. I'd like you to create this.

Scott: Thanks very much for considering me. This is obviously important, but could I get back to you about it later this afternoon – say at 3:00 p.m.?

Laura: Sure, that will be fine. Let's meet in my office then.

Scott's response was just right. He has bought time to check whether there's any way he can fit the new assignment into his schedule, without showing disrespect or losing his manager's approval.

Effective Time Management

Once Scott has consulted his schedule carefully, though, he realizes that he just can't take on more work. So he prepares a suitable response.

Scott meets his manager at 3:00 p.m. Follow along with their discussion.

Scott: At the moment, I'm working on the campaign for Easy Nomad Travel. Our deadline is the end of next week, and I'm worried that we might miss this if I take time out to work on the portfolio. If we don't do a good job, I'm afraid we'll lose further business from the client. What do you think?

Laura: Yes, I see what you mean. I'm tracking everything for that campaign, and I know there's still a lot of ground to cover.

Scott: Also, I'm just not sure I'll do the best job on the portfolio. I don't know all that much about Gleeson Associates.

Laura: Well that's easy to remedy. Here's the file I've put together. Why don't you take it and have a look?

This time, Scott started out well. He made it clear to his manager exactly why it would be a bad idea for him to take on new work – it could compromise his work for an existing client.

He also avoided being abrupt or dictating to his manager. Instead he threw the ball into her court by asking for her thoughts.

However, Scott also made a mistake.

Question

What did Scott do wrong in his second discussion with his manager?

Options:

1. He failed to promote his skills to his manager, instead admitting he might not do a good job

2. He opened the way for a discussion of whether he should take on the new work

3. He failed to say the word "no" clearly and unambiguously

Answer:

Option 1: This is an incorrect option. It's more important that Scott has the time to complete his work properly than for him to "sell" his abilities to his manager.

Option 2: This is the correct option. Scott should have left things where they were after his initial explanation of his concerns. Instead, he made the mistake of inviting a discussion about his suitability for taking on the job.

Option 3: This option is incorrect. It's disrespectful to respond to a manager's request with an abrupt "no." In fact, Scott did the right thing in his opening – without using the word "no," he made it clear to his manager why he shouldn't take on the new work.

Now it has become tricky for Scott to insist that he absolutely can't afford to take on more work.

Instead, he could have offered a helpful suggestion to close the discussion effectively. He might have said something like "Have you considered asking Tom to compile the portfolio? He has been doing some great work."

Or, instead of volunteering someone else's time, Scott could have ended with an offer to assist whoever does take on the job. This would be a good way to soften his refusal to accept work he doesn't have the time to complete.

Question

Effective Time Management

As the leader of a team facing a tough deadline, Patrick's schedule for the next few weeks is completely full. Patrick's manager asks him to take on the work of another team leader, who is due to go on leave in two days.

In which way would it be best for Patrick to respond?

Options:

1. "No way, I simply can't do that. I'm already extremely busy and I can't afford to take on more work."

2. "I'm glad you feel I could manage Tim's team. However, I won't then be able to ensure that my team meets its deadlines. Maria, who's on Tim's team, is very professional. Have you considered asking her?"

3. "Well, I'm not sure. I have an awful lot of work to complete if my own team is going to meet its deadline next week. Do you really think I'll be able to manage?"

4. "Sure. I'll be happy to help. I'll make the time somehow."

Answer:

Option 1: This option is incorrect. This is too abrupt and it's disrespectful of the authority Patrick's manager has. Patrick needs to refuse the additional work, but without causing offense or sounding insubordinate.

Option 2: This is the correct option. It's best for Patrick to indicate that he's happy to have been asked to assume more responsibility, but to make it clear that doing this would force him to compromise his key responsibilities. Ending with a helpful suggestion, rather than inviting further discussion, is also an effective approach.

Option 3: This is an incorrect option. Patrick should avoid inviting discussion about whether he's able to do the additional work. This may result in his being talked into accepting work he already knows he doesn't have the time to complete.

Option 4: This option is incorrect. It's inappropriate for Patrick to accept the new work if he knows he won't have time to complete it properly or to meet his existing responsibilities if he does.

Question

Three weeks later, Patrick's manager asks him to compile a detailed report comparing the team's output for the year so far with its output from the previous year. Patrick doubts he has the time to take on the work. Before giving a final answer, he wants to buy some time.

Which is the most appropriate response?

Options:

1. "That sounds like a useful report to have. Can I think about it and get back to you this afternoon – say at 2:00 p.m.?"

2. "I'll think about it."

3. "Um. Well. I'm not sure about this. Can we talk about what's happening with the new campaign my team has taken on for now?"

Answer:

Option 1: This is the correct option. Patrick should indicate that he takes the request seriously but needs more time to think about it. This will give him time to determine whether he can fit more work into his schedule and, if it's clear he can't, to prepare his response.

Option 2: This is an incorrect option. Just saying "I'll think about it" is a little abrupt and too ambiguous. Patrick should give his manager a deadline for when he will let him know. Overall, this response sounds

Effective Time Management

discourteous and isn't an appropriate way to answer a request from a manager.

Option 3: This option is incorrect. Instead of appearing uncertain or trying to change the subject, Patrick should simply ask for more time to think about the request before giving a final response.

HANDLING DISRUPTIVE PHONE CALLS

Handling disruptive phone calls

You've blocked off exactly two hours to create an accounting spreadsheet. Next, a colleague comes to ask your advice about a software error. Your phone rings and it's an important client on the other end. And you notice that an e-mail marked urgent has arrived in your inbox.

For most people, an important part of work life is interacting with others. Breaks and socializing with colleagues are important too – sometimes you need time away from your desk.

But have you ever considered how much time you spend handling interruptions?

These can eat into the time you need to spend getting your work done, making you less productive and more stressed.

In a typical office, interruptions come from a variety of sources:

- managers asking for updates, making new work requests, or popping in to discuss developments informally,

Effective Time Management

- colleagues who request assistance or just want to chat,
- meetings, which are often overly long and sometimes unnecessary,
- your telephone and cell phone, with calls from fellow employees, clients, family members, or friends,
- your e-mail, with messages ranging from urgent work requests to greetings or jokes from friends, and
- noise from nearby colleagues and their telephones.

Even if some of the interruptions you listed on the previous page are brief, they can still rob you of a lot of time. This is because after you've dealt with an interruption, you typically need extra time to regain your focus on what you were doing before. You can think of this as "switching" time – it almost always takes some time to switch between tasks.

If you were part-way through adding a set of sales figures, for example, you'll probably have to return to the top and start again.

And if you were in the middle of writing a report, you'll need to regain your concentration and reread the last few paragraphs you wrote before you continue.

Some straightforward strategies can help you to minimize interruptions at work. You can use voice mail to prevent phone calls from disrupting your work. And you can close your e-mail while you're completing a task. If you have your own office space, close your door and possibly even post a "do not disturb" sign on it until you've finished what has to be done.

Whenever necessary, you should be direct with managers or colleagues. If you don't have enough time to chat or assist with a problem, say so.

Mentioning what it is you need to finish can help keep this from sounding too abrupt.

Among the most time consuming of interruptions when you're working are phone calls. When you can't simply turn on your answering machine, you can use other strategies for reducing the time you spend handling phone calls. These include delegating the calls to others, shortening the durations of calls, and, when necessary, rescheduling them for a time when you're less busy.

Explore each strategy for minimizing phone call interruptions for more information.

Delegating

If you receive a call when you're busy, it may be appropriate to delegate the call by redirecting it to someone else.

To do this without causing offense, you can offer to put the caller through to someone who's better equipped to deal with the relevant query or problem.

Shortening the calls

Often, you can shorten the time a call takes by letting the caller know there's a deadline involved. For example, you might state up front that you have an appointment in 15 minutes but will do your best to resolve the caller's query in that time.

Follow-up calls may not be required because setting a time limit encourages a caller to come straight to the point.

Rescheduling

If you're too busy to handle a call, it may be appropriate to reschedule it. However, it's important to do this without suggesting that you're dismissing the importance of the caller's concerns.

Generally, you should offer a brief explanation of why you're not available to talk – a pressing appointment, for example – and offer times at which you will be available.

When you use one of the strategies for minimizing the time a phone call takes, it's important to avoid being rude or too abrupt.

Consider how you'd feel as the caller if the person who answered said something like "Not now, I'm busy. Call me again in three hours."

This is an example of rescheduling a call, but it's likely to leave the caller offended and dissatisfied. A better response would be "I'm afraid I'm in the middle of something rather urgent. Could I call you back, say at 3:00 p.m.?"

Say you're in the middle of drafting a proposal when you receive a call from your company's Accounts Department. There's a query about some figures and getting to the bottom of it is likely to be time consuming. To make your own work deadline, you can choose to delegate or shorten the call, or to reschedule it.

See each strategy for an example of how you can respond to the caller.

Delegate

"I'm a bit pressed at the moment, but it would be a good idea for you to talk to Jim, who compiled those figures for us. He can give you better information. Can I transfer you to him?"

Shorten the call

"I've pulled out the figures and will go over them with you now, but I'm afraid I've got only 20 minutes. If there's anything more to cover, let's schedule a call for later this afternoon."

Reschedule

"I've got an appointment now, but I'll be available from 3:00 p.m. and again first thing tomorrow morning. Can I call you at either of those times?"

Question

Sandra is in the middle of a complex set of calculations when her phone rings. The caller is a supplier who needs help completing a form.

In which ways is it appropriate for Sandra to respond to minimize the time that the call takes?

Options:

1. "I'm busy now. You'll have to find someone else to help you."

2. "I'm afraid I'm tied up at the moment, but can I call you back — either today after lunch or first thing tomorrow?"

3. "I'm happy to help, but I'm afraid I've got only 15 minutes free now. Let's go over what's required, and we can set up another call if that's not enough time."

4. "I'm in the middle of a tricky calculation. It's not a great time for me."

5. "I'm not the best person to help — can I put you through to Becky? She knows exactly what's required."

Answer:

Option 1: This option is incorrect. Although it may be appropriate to reschedule the call, it's important to do this without being abrupt or dismissive of the caller.

Option 2: This is a correct option. It's appropriate to reschedule a call if you're too busy to take it. In this case, it can help to offer the caller choices about when it would be convenient to talk again.

Option 3: This option is correct. Giving a caller a time limit is a good way of shortening the likely duration of a call.

Option 4: This is an incorrect option. It would be rude simply to tell a caller that you're in the middle of something else. The caller may be offended.

Option 5: This option is correct. One way to minimize the interruption is to delegate the call by redirecting it to someone else qualified to handle it.

Sometimes a particular client or customer calls often and requires frequent reassurance. These calls can take up a lot of time and even prevent you from giving enough attention to other clients.

If you cut the calls short, you may risk offending or even losing the client.

And if you continue to spend more time on the calls than you have, you're at risk of falling behind in your work.

There are two main things you can do to help prevent regular calls from a client from disrupting your work:
- pre-empt the calls and phone the client yourself when you have the time, and
- specify the times when you're available to accept and return calls so that the client knows what to expect – and use voice mail to do this when you're not available.

Say a client calls you several times during the week. To minimize disruptions to your work, you can plan to call the client yourself each Monday morning. You can also tell the client when you're free to take calls – for instance, before 10:00 a.m. or after 3:00 p.m. each day.

Question

David, who's in charge of customer support for a company that sells and services photocopy machines, is working on an urgent report when his phone rings. It's a colleague in another department who wants to go over customer complaints received over the last three months.

Which responses would it be appropriate for David to make?

Options:

1. "I'm actually not the best person for this. Can I put you through to Alison? She can give you all the information we have."

2. "Now's not a good time."

3. "It's not important that you have this information now, but it is important that I finish my report – it's

due in by the end of the day. Please call me tomorrow."

4. "I'm afraid I'm tied up at the moment. Can I call you back? How's after lunch today, or would first thing tomorrow be better?"

5. "I'm happy to help, but I've got only ten minutes now. I'll give you what I can, and we can talk again later if necessary."

Answer:

Option 1: This option is correct. One way to manage calls you don't have time to deal with is to delegate them to others who are suitably qualified.

Option 2: This option is incorrect. Just saying that it's not a good time or that you're busy is too abrupt. The caller may be offended.

Effective Time Management

Option 3: This is an incorrect option. It's unprofessional and impolite to undermine the importance of a caller's query, whether the caller is a customer or a colleague.

Option 4: This option is correct. It's appropriate to reschedule the call for a time when you'll be less busy and more able to focus on assisting the caller.

Option 5: This is a correct option. Setting a clear time limit for the call is an effective way to shorten the conversation and encourage the caller to stay focused.

Question

David ends the call with his colleague, but then his phone rings again. This time it's a customer who often calls with what seem like trivial questions about his service contract. David then has to spend up to 20 minutes on the phone instead of continuing with his work.

In which ways would it be appropriate for David to deal with the customer?

Options:

1. Let the customer know exactly when he's available to take calls

2. Politely ask the customer to stop calling unless there's a real problem

3. Spend as long as necessary reassuring the customer each time he calls

4. Call the customer once a week to check that he's happy with the service he's receiving

Answer:

Option 1: This is a correct option. David should inform the customer when he's available to take and return calls so that the customer knows what to expect.

Option 2: This option is incorrect. It would be impolite and unprofessional to suggest that the customer's calls aren't important.

Option 3: This is an incorrect option. If the customer's calls aren't about urgent problems and they're preventing David from completing work that's important, he should take steps to minimize the time they take.

Option 4: This option is correct. A good strategy for handling customers or clients who call often is to pre-empt their calls. That way, David is more in control of how long he can spend on the phone.

HANDLING DROP-IN VISITORS

Handling drop-in visitors

As a manager, Nina has an open-door policy. She knows it's important that her staff can come to her with any problems. In practice though, Nina spends so much time dealing with drop-in visitors that she's struggling to get her own work done.

Drop-in visitors are people who come into your office or to see you at your desk without a prior appointment. They can include managers, coworkers, customers or vendors, and friends.

Sometimes drop-in visitors want your help with problems or to discuss work-related issues. At other times, they may stop by just to chat. They can use up some of your valuable time.

No matter how many visitors you have, you need to get your own work done.

Several strategies can help you reduce the time you spend dealing with drop-in visitors. You can set a time limit on visits, limit the times you're available, immediately ask any visitor how you can help, and encourage visits outside your workplace.

Explore each strategy for more information about how to minimize the time you spend with drop-in visitors.

Set time limits

Sometimes a drop-in visitor may settle in to chat or take a long time getting to a point. Setting a time limit on the discussion is a good way to prevent this. For example, you might say something like, "Hi Tim, come in. I've got just ten or so minutes right now, but how can I help?"

If the time you've set for a discussion proves insufficient, you can schedule another time when you'll be less busy for continuing the discussion.

Limit times you're available

If you're a manager, it's important to make time to see staff who need your assistance. But it's also important that you have enough time to complete your own work. You could choose to make it clear that you're available only between certain times – for example, between 2:00 and 4:00 p.m. each day.

You could also choose to limit the issues you're available to discuss. For instance, you could ask staff to keep all nonurgent questions until a weekly meeting that's scheduled for Monday mornings.

Ask how you can help

If you ask how you can help as soon as a drop-in visitor arrives at your desk, it shows that you're expecting the visitor to address a work-related issue. Visitors who were hoping just to chat are likely to get the message that if you're busy at your desk, it means another time – like when you're obviously taking a lunch break – would be better for socializing.

Asking how you can help will also prompt a visitor who wants to address a work-related issue to come straight to the point, which can save time.

Encourage visits outside your workplace

You should also ask friends or colleagues who want to catch up socially to meet you outside the workplace – for instance, during lunch breaks or after work hours.

In addition, it often helps to pre-empt visits. If you're a manager, you can schedule time to make the rounds and find out if any team members need your help – rather than facing interruptions once you're focusing on your own work.

If you're too busy to deal with unexpected visitors, you should say so directly. You can do this without being abrupt. An example might be "I'm afraid I've got an important report due. Unless it's urgent, could we meet later, say at 3:00 p.m.?"

Colleagues are likely to understand and empathize if you're trying to get your work done, and you'll be able to focus better on speaking to them once you know you've got the time.

Ultimately, minimizing interruptions during the time you've scheduled to get your own work done will help your career. It will also leave you less stressed, with time left to assist others and to relax once your work is done.

Question

Keith, a manager, is often part-way through a task when one of the staff members on his team pops into his office, either to ask for assistance or to pass on the latest gossip.

In which ways is it appropriate for Keith to respond?

Options:

1. Let staff members know that he's available daily from 2:00 to 4:00 p.m.

2. When a staff member arrives in his office, specify that he has 15 minutes free to talk

3. Ask staff members who often drop in to socialize to meet him during a lunch break instead

4. E-mail all staff members asking them not to bother him

5. Point out to staff members who drop by that they should be getting their work done without assistance

6. Immediately ask any staff member who arrives in his office how he can help

Answer:

Option 1: This is a correct option. It's a good idea for Keith to limit the times at which it's known he's available. Then at other times, he can focus on completing his own work.

Option 2: This option is correct. Setting a time limit on each visit – without being abrupt or impolite – will give Keith more time to finish his own work.

Option 3: This option is correct. Keith should encourage visitors – especially those who just want to chat – to meet him outside the workplace or outside work hours, rather than when he's focused on getting his own work done.

Option 4: This option is incorrect. Although Keith should limit the times for which he's available, he shouldn't prevent his staff from contacting him at all.

Option 5: This is an incorrect option. This response sends a message that you don't want to be bothered with employees. It would be unwise for a manager to earn a reputation for being unfriendly and unsupportive.

Option 6: This is a correct option. By asking a drop-in visitor how he can help, Keith will make it clear that he expects the purpose of the visit to be work-related. He'll also encourage the visitor to come to the point quickly.

REFERENCES

References
Taking Control with Time Management, 5th Edition - 2004, M.J. Weeks and Janis Fisher Chan
Time Management: Increase Your Personal Productivity and Effectiveness - 2005, Harvard Business School Publishing, Harvard Business Press
Creative Time Management for the New Millennium - 1999, Dr. Jan Yager, Hannacroix Creek Books
The 80/20 Principle: The Secret of Achieving More with Less -1998, Richard Koch, Nicholas Brealey Publishing
Time Management: Proven Techniques For Making Every Minute Count, Second Edition - 2008, Richard Walsh, Adams Media
Taking Control with Time Management, 5th Edition - 2004, M.J. Weeks and Janis Fisher Chan
Successful Time Management for Dummies - 2009, Dirk Zeller, John Wiley & Sons

GLOSSARY

Glossary
B
body clock - The natural cycle of waking, sleep, and alertness that governs the way that individuals can perform tasks. Also referred to as the energy cycle or circadian rhythm.
C
circadian rhythm - The natural cycle of waking, sleep, and alertness that governs the way that individuals can perform tasks. Also referred to as the energy cycle and the body clock.
E
energy cycle - The natural cycle of waking, sleep, and alertness that governs the way that individuals can perform tasks. Also referred to as circadian rhythm or the body clock.
extravert - Used in the context of the Myers-Briggs personality type indicator test, an extravert gains energy from interacting with people and prefers spending his or her time focusing on people and things.

F
feeler - Used in the context of the Myers-Briggs personality type indicator test, a feeler prefers to make decisions based on personal concerns and the needs of the people involved in the context of the decision.

I
introvert - Used in the context of the Myers-Briggs personality type indicator test, an introvert gains energy from spending time alone and focuses on the inner world of concepts and ideas.

intuitor - Used in the context of the Myers-Briggs personality type indicator test, an intuitor is someone who prefers to gather information through the identification of patterns and considering possibilities from the information received.

J
judger - Used in the context of the Myers-Briggs personality type indicator test, a judger prefers a more structured way of interacting with the world and often appears very organized or rigid.

M
Myers-Briggs personality type indicator test - This personality measure differentiates between 16 personality types according to a person's preferences for how they acquire energy, how they take in information, how they make decisions, and how they interact with the external world.

P
perceiver - Used in the context of the Myers-Briggs personality type indicator test, a perceiver prefers a flexible or adaptable way of interacting with the world and may often appear easy-going or disorganized.

S

sensor - Used in the context of the Myers-Briggs personality type indicator test, a sensor is someone who prefers to gather physical information using his or her five senses, paying attention to details and physical reality.

T

thinker - Used in the context of the Myers-Briggs personality type indicator test, a thinker prefers to make decisions based on objective principles, general rules, and facts.

time logs - Time logs are used to record the amount of time spent on tasks during a day. They include the time spent, the activity category, and the activity priority. They are used to audit the time spent in a typical day.

www.ingramcontent.com/pod-product-compliance
Lightning Source LLC
Chambersburg PA
CBHW020919180526
45163CB00007B/2804